Spanish Phonetics and Phonemics

Present. cap 16

Spanish Phonetics and Phonemics

by

HANS-JÖRG BUSCH

and

TOM LATHROP

LINGUATEXT, LTD.
NEWARK, DELAWARE

270 Indian Road
Newark, Delaware 19711
(302) 453-8695
www.LinguaTextLtd.com

MANUFACTURED IN THE UNITED STATES OF AMERICA

ISBN: 0-942566-44-0

Table of Contents

Preface

IF THIS IS YOUR FIRST experience with a course of a linguistic nature, most everything will be new to you—new terminology, new concepts, and most particularly, new language sounds to master. But don't worry.

We have had a lot of experience teaching Spanish pronunciation to American students at the college level, and we also remember what it was like when we were learning this material ourselves. One of us learned Spanish phonetics in Germany and the other in California, and we recall our struggle through the new material. In our teaching over the years, we have learned how to get good results by simplifying the course rather than complicating it, thus we have produced a condensed book which we hope will be easy to study and learn from. We also have prepared and included a CD of exercises that follow the book's printed exercises for you to work with.

We cannot emphasize enough how important it is to pronounce well. If your word-order is great and you have lots of vocabulary, but your pronunciation is bad, it will undermine your audience's opinion about your language competence and in your abilities in general. On the other hand, if your pronunciation is excellent, but your other two skills are not as good, you can still communicate your message in simpler terms—simple and direct is, after all, laudable trait—and inspire confidence in yourself and your linguistic ability.

Mastering pronunciation is quite a bit like mastering a musical instrument. You can learn enough about playing the guitar in a semester, enough to accompany yourself in a number of songs, but to play at the level of a concert musician or as a studio player requires many years of lessons and practice.

This course is like that first semester of learning a musical instrument. If at the end of this semester you will have learned well and applied your knowledge to your speaking of Spanish, and if you travel very soon to a Spanish-speaking country, we hope that the reaction of people in that country will be: "I can tell you are not a native speaker of Spanish, but where are you from?" This will mean that you have rid yourself of the "American accent," which is a pretty big accomplishment. Whereas a French accent in English may be charming, an American accent in Spanish sounds dreadful.

After you practice for a long time and get really good in pronunciation, you might be met with a reaction such as: "What Spanish-speaking country are you from?" meaning that they think you are native, but not from the country you are in.

The third level, to be mistaken for a native of the country you are in, requires complete mastery of even the smallest nuances of pronunciation and intonation. At the end of this course you will be pretty far from that goal, but a solid foundation will go a long way towards this eventual mastery.

At the same time that you improve your pronunciation of Spanish, we hope you will enjoy watching the phonetic nature of the language unfold, and will learn some important linguistic concepts along the way.

We have written this book in English because there are too many new concepts and too much new vocabulary to confuse things by writing in Spanish. We give the Spanish equivalents of all the technical vocabulary, so if the course is conducted in Spanish you'll have the words you need.

We would like to thank the speakers in the audio program, both from Colombia, Dora and Alberto Delgado. We also thank Francisco Aragón-Guiller who found the newspaper texts used in exercises.

If you have any comments don't hesitate to get in touch with either of us: leipzig@udel.edu or lathrop@udel.edu.

H.-J. B.
T. A. L.

Newark, Delaware
September, 2005

1
Syllabification in Spanish

WORD-PROCESSING PROGRAMS WORK beautifully for dividing syllables and putting hyphens in the right place in Spanish. If it's all so automatic, why should you learn how to do it manually? It's important because, for example, variations in vowel quality—and you'll learn what this is pretty soon—often depend on how a syllable ends. If it is an OPEN SYLLABLE (that is, if the syllable *ends in a vowel*), that vowel will be pronounced one way) and if it's a CLOSED SYLLABLE (that is, if the syllable *ends in a consonant*) it'll be pronounced another way. Try this little experiment to see how open and closed syllables affect pronunciation: the word **dolor** has two **o**s and two syllables. The first syllable, **do-**, is open, and the **o** is pronounced one way. The second syllable, **-lor**, is closed, and the **o** is pronounced another way. Another reason you should learn how to divide words into syllables is to know where to stress a word, and whether or not you have to use a written accent.

Before we describe how to divide syllables, we must first define what a syllable is.

Words are made of syllables (**stu-dent, u-ni-ver-si-ty**). Some words are just one syllable long (**go, be**). In English, syllables can vary in length from one to nine letters: **I, me, eat, high, fifth, height, thought, strength, strengths**. The major characteristic of any syllable is that there is just one vowel sound (or diphthong, which is a combination of two vowel sounds[1]), but there can be from one to four consonants in a Spanish syllable. Indeed, some syllables are made of a vowel and nothing more, as the underlined letters show in these words: **a-yer, po-e-ta, ca-í**. Most of the time, one or more consonants can precede the vowel (**la-go, co-mí, bra-zo, pla-za, sal-dré**), or follow it (**ar-te, en-tre, ins-tan-te**), and one or more consonants can precede and follow the vowel sound (**can-tar, a-la-crán, ac-triz, trans-crip-ción**).

---

[1] We'll get into diphthongs in the next lesson.

Spanish syllables, as well as words, can begin with any letter of the Spanish alphabet (**a-ma, ban-ca, ca-ma, chis-te, da-ma, es-tar, fin**, and so on); certain consonant clusters of two consonants (all of them ending in either **-l** or **-r**) can begin them as well: **pre-mio, bra-zo, tra-er, dra-ma, cre-er, gran-de, frí-o, plan, blan-co, cla-ro, glo-bo, fla-co**. If the consonant cluster doesn't end with **-l** or **–r**, it cannot begin a syllable.

Unlike syllable division in English, where the computer is sometimes baffled,[2] rules for dividing Spanish words are very exact. Here are the rules you need to know.

Where there is an alternation of vowels and consonants, syllables divide between the vowel and the consonant:

o-re-ja	**fo-né-ti-ca**
nú-me-ro	**re-no-va-da**
co-mu-ni-ca-do	**co-mer**

Where there are *two* consonants between vowels, there are two rules:

1. If there is cluster with the sounds **p,t,k**[3]**,b,d,g,f** + **l** or **r**, the syllable breaks before the consonant cluster:

de-trás	**o-fre-ce**	**co-pla**

2. Any *other* cluster of two consonants breaks between the two consonants:

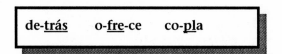

[2] For example, the word present in English is divided two different ways depending on its function. As a verb it's **pre-sent** *(I'll present my findings at the meeting)*, and as a noun it's **pres-ent** *(Here is a present for you)*. Today's computerized hyphenation programs just aren't sophisticated enough to tell the difference so they choose one solution for both words (thus they syllabify those words wrong half the time).

[3] We use **k** here and elsewhere to represent that sound when spelled **c** as in *crema, comer, quién, qué,* since *c* has another pronunciation as well, as in *cena, cine*.

cam-po	**al-go**
ac-ción	**es-tar**
car-ne	**bur-la**
in-sis-te	**has-ta**

If there are *three or more* consonants, the same rules apply. If a **p, t, k, b, d, g, f + r, l** cluster ends the group of consonants, the syllable breaks **BEFORE** that cluster:

con-flu-yente	**cum-plir**
mal-cria-do	**trans-cri-to**

Where there are three or four consonants together and the second one is an **s**, syllables always divide *after* the **s**:

ins-tante	**cons-trucción**
sols-ticio	**trans-ductor**

You have to be careful about dividing Spanish syllables this way because English tends to break words like these *before* the **s**: **per-spective, con-stitute.**

A special note about **x**: The letter **x**, typically represents **k-s** when between vowels, and can represent either **k-s** or just the sound **s** before a consonant, depending how the speaker feels. But no matter how **x** is pronounced *before a consonant*, the syllable divides after it: **ex-tra, ex-periencia.** *Between vowels*, you have to treat **x** as if it were **k-s** and divide the syllables after the **k-**. In fact, when you do phonetic transcriptions at the end of this course, you'll have to rewrite the word with **k-s**: **taxi**

= **tak-si, ortodoxo = or-to-dok-so.**[4]

Spanish syllables *always* break before **ch, ll, ñ** and **rr** either between vowels or when another consonant precedes (a consonant can't precede **rr** or **ñ**):

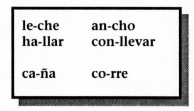

le-che	**an-cho**
ha-llar	**con-llevar**
ca-ña	**co-rre**

A consonant that ends a word is a part of the final syllable:

pa-<u>pel</u>	fá-<u>cil</u>

If there is ever a doubt as to where to break syllables in words with two or more consonants between vowels, here is a sure-fire alternate system:

Look at the combination of consonants after the vowels.

If they can start a word, then the syllable breaks right after the vowel. If they cannot start a word, add the first consonant to the previous vowel.

If the remaining consonant or consonants can start a word, you have found the beginning of the next syllable, if not, continue adding consonants to the previous syllable until the remaining consonant or group of consonants can start a word.

---

[4] Of course, to *hyphenate* words like ***taxi*** in writing, you must divide them before the **-x-**: **ta-xi.**

Example: CONTRASTE

NTR	No, words cannot start with NTR-.
TR:	Yes, words can start with TR-.
	∴ **The first syllable is *con*-.**
ST:	No, words cannot start with ST-.
T:	Yes, words can start with T-.
	∴ **The second syllable is *–tras*- and the last syllable is *–te*.**

Here is another example:

Example: SOLSTICIO

LST: No, words cannot start with LST-.
ST: No, words cannot start with ST-.
T: Yes, words can start with T-.
∴ **The first syllable is *sols*-. The second syllable is -*ti*- and the third *–cio*.**

DIPHTHONGS AND TRIPHTHONGS

Two vowel sounds in the *same* syllable are known as a DIPHTHONG (note the "*phth*" spelling). One of these sounds, at least in Spanish, is always [y] as in **yellow** (spelled *i* or *y*) or [w] as in **well** (overwhelmingly spelled **u**, but there are a *few* foreign words unavoidably spelled with **w**, such as **Washington**); and the other vowel sound is a full vowel [a,e,i,o,u]. The [y] and [w] sounds are called GLIDES because, they move—they *glide*—to or from the position where the full vowel is articulated. These glides are also called *semi-vowels*.

hac<u>ia</u>	superfic<u>ie</u>	rec<u>io</u>
ten<u>ue</u>	rec<u>ua</u>	c<u>iu</u>dad

Diphthongs are treated as normal vowels for purposes of division of syllables:

c*ua*n-do	***sie*n-do**	**c*ue*n-to**
b*ui*-tre	**v*iu*-da**	**vir-t*uo*-sa**

When **u** and **i** are together, the first one is the semi-vowel and the *second* one is the full vowel:

cuidado	**ciudad**

If two vowels are together and neither one is an **i** or a **u**, *each one* is the nucleus of its own syllable:

Amade-o	**te-atro**

When an **i** or a **u** is in contact with another vowel, and there is a written accent on the **í** or **ú**, both vowels are part of separate syllables:

frí-o	**tí-a**	**(que) varí-en**
dú-o	**(el) actú-a**	**la-ú-des**

A TRIPHTHONG (again, note the *"phth"* spelling) is three vowel sounds in the same syllable. Triphthongs *begin and end* with **i (y)** or **u***:*

miau	**Uruguay**
Paraguay	**semiautomático**
buey	

Pa-ra-noi-a
pa-ra-no-ía?

Words like **playa** don't have a triphthong because the conditions aren't met—here, the *first* and *last* vowels are **a**, so the word divides regularly before the diphthong: **pla-ya.** Don't be fooled by the presence of *four* unaccented vowels in a row—there's *never* a triphthong in these cases, and the syllables always break between the two diphthongs:

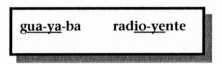

gua-ya-ba **radio-yente**

Our observation at the beginning of the lesson that "a syllable must have one vowel" should now read: *"a syllable must have one vowel, diphthong, or triphthong."*

EXERCISE

Break into syllables. Rewrite those words with an **x** (using **k-s**) where necessary.

a b s t e n e r
a é r e o
a f e a r
a l b e d r í o
a n c h o a
a p e o
a p i o
B a b i e c a
b a l n e a r i o
b e o d o
b i s i e s t o
b o x e o
c a e r
c a l l e
c a m b i o
C a s i l d e a
c i r c u n s t a n c i a
c o e x i s t e
c o i n c i d e

c o j e o
c o n s t a b a
C o n s t a n z a
c o n s t e l a c i o n e s
c o n s t e r n a r
c o n s t i t u c i o n a l
c o n s t i t u i d a
c o n s t r u c c i ó n
c o n s t r u i d o
c o n s t r u i r
c r í e
d a l i a
d e i f i c a r
d e l e i t e
d e l i r i o
d e r r o c a r
d e s c u i d a d o
d e s e o
d e s h a c e r

d e u d a
e g o í s m o
e m p e o r a
e n f r í o
e n v í o
e s t a d o u n i d e n s e
e x a c t o
e x a m e n
f í e n
f r a s e o l o g í a
h e r o í n a
h i n c h a r
i n c o n s t a n t e
i n t e r s t i c i o
i n s t a l a
i n s t a n t e
i n s t a r
i n s t i l a r
i n s t i n t o
i n s t i t u c i ó n
i n s t r u c t o r
i n s t r u m e n t o
j a e z
l e í b l e
l l e n a r
l o a b l e
m a g i a
m a l c r i a d o
m o n s t r u o
o b o e
p a r a n o i a
p o e m a
r e c o n s t i t u c i ó n
r e i n s t a l a r
r e m e d i o
r e s i d u o
r e t r o a c t i v o
r u i d o
r u i n no tilde
s o e z
s o i s
s o l s t i c i o
s o n r e i r á
s u p e r s t i c i ó n
t e í s m o
t r a n s d u c t o r
t r i u n f a
t u i c i ó n
v e i n t i u n o
v í d e o

coexiste

río

reúno (reunir) • re-ú-no

• reu nir

2
Stress: When is an Accent Necessary?

SPANISH HAS PERFECTED a spelling system so that you can tell where a word is stressed, whether or not it has an accent on it (assuming the word is correctly written!). Most words don't have an accent on them because they fall into one of two overwhelmingly common categories.[1]

When you see a Spanish word *without a written accent,* look at the last letter to find out where it is stressed.

CATEGORY 1: If the word *ends in a vowel or a diphthong* (except one with final **y**—see the next page) is it stressed on the PENULT (next-to-last syllable).[2] Words with this kind of stress are called *LLANAS* in Spanish. The letter in italics shows the stress:

caball*e*ro	*ca*sa	*ce*sta
*co*me	diam*a*nte	h*a*bla
mos*ta*za	*ta*xi	*tri*bu
superf*i*cie	cont*i*nuo	h*a*cia

Llanos

[1] In an unscientific survey, we counted the words from a Uruguayan newspaper article. There were 264 words and only 19 of them had accents on them. That's only 7.2% with accents. You can see that the two common categories cover the great majority of words.

[2] To be complete, we should say a couple more things: if a word *ends in a triphthong,* it is stressed on the last syllable with no accent: **Paraguay, Uruguay.**

Now, since some conjugated forms end in **-s** and **-n**, and because plurals of nouns and adjectives also end in **-s**, always with *no change in stress,* the rule has to be refined a bit: "If the word without a written accent ends in a **vowel,** ***n,*** or ***s*** it is stressed on the penult."

h*a*blo	c*o*mo	desc*u*bro	clase	cont*i*nuo
h*a*bla	c*o*me	desc*u*bre	clases	cont*i*nuos
h*a*blas	c*o*mes	desc*u*bres	t*a*xi	tr*i*bu
h*a*blan	c*o*men	desc*u*bren	t*a*xis	tr*i*bus

CATEGORY 2: If a word without a written accent ends in a consonant (but not **-n** or **-s**, of course), the word is stressed on the last syllable. **Y** is also included in this list. Words that are stressed on the last syllable are called AGUDAS in Spanish:

color	costal	ciudad	avestruz
reloj	deber	estoy	maguey

Written accents are guided by spelling, not pronunciation. For example, even though final **-s** and final **-z** sound the same in Latin American Spanish, **crisis** has no accent, but **lápiz** does. Similarly, some people don't pronounce the final **-d** in **ciudad**—still, there is no written accent. Although the **j** in **reloj** isn't pronounced, it still has no written accent. **Ahinco** 'insistence' and **mohino** 'mournful', where the vowel and **i** are separated by an **h,** also have no accent (they are syllabified counting the silent **h** as a normal consonant, even though it isn't pronounced: **a-hin-co, mo-hi-no**).

EXCEPTIONS TO CATEGORIES 1 AND 2: All exceptions bear a written accent. Exceptions are, simply, those words ending in a **vowel, n, s** which are stressed somewhere *other than* the next-to-last syllable, or words ending in a **consonant** (not **n** or **s**) which are stressed anywhere *other than* the last syllable:

EXCEPTIONS TO CATEGORY 1:

maravedí	Perú	canté	condición
esdrújula	dímelo	maletín	cortés

EXCEPTIONS TO CATEGORY 2:

difícil	tórax	mármol	albímar
árbol	Martínez	mármol	carácter

Some words, because of these rules, take an accent in the plural form where there is none in the singular, and vice-versa: **joven, jóvenes; maletín, maletines, condición, condiciones.**

It goes without saying (even though we're saying it) that since the rules for unaccented words cover only those that are stressed on the last or next-to-last syllables, any word stressed on the ANTEPENULT (= three syllable back) needs a written accent. Words stressed on the antepenult are called ESDRÚJULAS in Spanish, a wonderful term, since "esdrújula" is an *esdrújula*:

académico	agrícola	básico
cámara	médico	cómico

Many people erroneously put an accent mark on words like **construido, huida, constituida**, but since these words obey the ordinary rules, accents are superfluous.

If two "strong" vowels are together (that is, any combination of **a, e, o**) the regular rules of stress apply:

c<u>ao</u>s	volv<u>eo</u>s	tr<u>ae</u>r	br<u>ea</u>

One syllable words don't have an accent (except to avoid confusion: **mi** vs **mí**, **de** vs. **dé**:[3]

fue	dio	guion	hui

Question words also require an accent, either in direct questions or indirect questions. A direct question is obvious: **¿Dónde está la llave?** An indirect question doesn't have a question mark, but still implies a question. **Ella me preguntó dónde estaba su llave.** Where no question is implied, there is no accent: **Ella me dijo donde estaba mi coche.**

It used to be that if a pronoun was attached to a verb form that had an accent on the last syllable, the accent was retained: **déme, despidióse**. The Royal Academy of the Language has now declared this is not the case anymore—regular accentuation rules apply: **deme, despidiose** The Academy further states that those demonstratives that act as pronouns no longer take an accent. What used to be **Voy a comprar éstos** is now **Voy a comprar estos.**

Although this goes against the rules of placing written accents, adverbs ending in **-mente** maintain any accent found on the base adjective: **explícita – explícitamente; fácil – fácilmente.**

Finally, there are only three Spanish nouns that change the syllable they are stressed on in the plural form: **carácter – caracteres, espécimen – especímenes, régimen – regímenes.**[4]

[3] The use of an accent on these short words that are spelled the same is far from capricious. **Mí** is a stressed word (**cerca de mí**) whereas **mi** is not **¿Dónde está mi coche?**)

[4] These three words are taken directly from Latin and obey Latin stress rules. Many speakers will pronounce the first of these **carácteres**, which eventually may become the standard pronunciation. This doesn't mean you should pronounce it that way.

EXERCISES

1. These words are stressed on the vowels in boldface. Write accents only over those words that need accents (and over the correct vowel)

Agustin	dorada
altar	dueña
anecdotas	ecos
angelicos	Eden
apice	epoca
aqui	especie
aristotelico	especifico.
armonia	esporadico
benevolas.	esquematico
biblico	esquematicos
celebre	esta
clerigo	estaticas
clerigos	estrecha
comun	etcetera
connotacion	etimologicas
construida	evalua
contemporanea	evangelica
deposito	exegesis
despues	explicitamente
dialectico	faciles
dialogo	figura
diferente	folklorico
dinamica	fonicamente

2 acentos prosódicos
Terminal en adverbio = mente : explícito
estrújula

adj + mente

régimen
regímenes (exception)
carácter
caracteres no stress
* adverbios are the only ones that have 2 acentos prosódicos. (natural stress + accent mark)

Aún no he dormido (yet)
Aun los que no estudiaron (even though) aprobaron

forja
formando
forzaran
frio
genericos
generos
gracias
Guillen
habil
hagiograficas
hermosa
heroes
historico
homericos
imagen
imagenes
impudico
instrumento
interes
inutilmente
jerarquico
judios
juridico
lana
latin
leon
linea
liquido
liturgicas
liturgico
llamas
logico
lugar
madre
mantener
Maria
martillo
martires
Menendez
merito
metaforas
metaforicas
miniaturas
monastica
mujer
ningun
nucleos
numero
ordenes
organo
Paraiso
patristica
piramide
poetico

dame : no tilde (new rule)
dámelo : si lleva
aún : si
[illegible] solo, sólo me

port**a**tiles
pres**e**ntes
proteg**i**do
p**u**blico
quiz**a**s
reci**e**n
recu**e**rda
rel**a**to
repres**e**nta
ret**o**ricos
rev**e**s
rom**a**nico
r**u**brica
sem**a**nticos
serm**o**n
simb**o**lica
simil**a**res

sit**u**a
sovi**e**tica
subr**a**ya
supl**i**ca
tambi**e**n
t**e**cnica
Teof**i**lo
teol**o**gica
te**o**logo
t**e**rminos
unica
util**i**sima
v**e**anse
veh**i**culo
v**i**rgenes
visi**o**n
vu**e**lve

2. Read the following text and place an accent when necessary. Boldface letters show where the stress is. We put an accent on **más** (because there is also a **mas** which means *but*).

"La Guantanamera"

"La Guantanam**e**ra" es **u**na de las canci**o**nes más fam**o**sas del m**u**ndo. El cant**a**nte haban**e**ro Jos**e**ito Fern**a**ndez la comp**u**so un inci**e**rto d**i**a de 1928. Era dur**a**nte el r**e**gimen de Ger**a**rdo Mach**a**do, **u**no de los l**i**deres de los reg**i**menes corr**u**ptos que se sucedi**e**ron **e**ntre mil novecientos trece y mil novecientos cincuenta e nueve en el pais. No soño con que medio siglo despues su cancion se convertiria en un autentico himno de Cuba. Joseito y "La Guantanamera" fueron, gracias al cantante norteamericano Pete Seeger, quien la popularizo en la decada de los sesenta, los precursores del gran boom internacion al que la musica popular cubana vive en nuestros dias.

Seeger penso que era una cancion de caracter folclorico. Le puso estrofas de varios "Versos sencillos" de Jose Marti—"Yo soy un hombre sincero/ de donde crece la palma/ y antes de morirme quiero/ echar mis versos del alma"—, y la cancion empezo a rodar por todo el mundo. Luego vinieron las versiones del trio californiano The Sandpippers y del frances Joe Dassin, y "La Guantanamera" se convirtio en una mina de oro.

Ajeno a este exito y a los derechos de autor, no fue hasta mil novecientos set enta y uno que Joseito Fernandez le pudo contar a Seeger la verdadera historia de la cancion. Joseito muri o el once de octubre de mil noveci entos setenta y nueve, sin ahorros ni lujos, aunque al menos su nombre quedo grabado en la historia de la musica cubana y mundial.

3
Spelling: Problem Letters

PEOPLE FREQUENTLY SAY THAT Spanish is a phonetic language, implying that if you can hear it, you can write it. This is largely true, but there are some problem sounds—sounds that can be spelled in different ways.

G, J, X

A **j** can appear before any vowel:

Before any vowel (J)

jamón	jerarquía	jinete
jorobado	jubilar	

A **g** when pronounced as a *jota*, can appear only before **e** and **i**:

G + e, i	gemir, Ginebra

So, in verbs that end in **-ger**, the **-g** changes to **j-** before **-a** and **-o**:

INFINITIVES ENDING IN -GER:	
escoger	escojo
escoge	escoja

But since **j** can appear before any vowel, in verbs whose infinitives end in **-jar**, the **j** is always kept before any vowel:

• ventaja
• Japon
generar
genético
geométrico
• Jerusalén
• joven
• judicial
• aconsejar
• coraje
• porcentaje (expeción)
• aprendisaje
• gigante
• gitana
• espionaje theoretically could be g. (excepción)

INFINITIVES ENDING IN -JAR

dejar	**deje**
manejar	**maneje**

Aside from this rule, there is no fool-proof answer to whether the *jota* sound before **e** and **i** is written with a **j** or a **g**, but there are several ways to make an educated guess.

Sometimes it helps to see if there is an English word that shares the same meaning. If there is one and it is written with a **j** or an **x**, then the Spanish word also has a **j**: **adjetivo** ('adjective'), **majestad** ('majesty'), subjetivo ('subjective'), **sujeto** ('subject'), **objetivo**('objective'), **ejemplo** ('example'), ejercicio ('exercise'), **ejecución** ('execution'). If it is written with a **g** in English, it might also be written with a **g** in Spanish: **género** ('gender'), **génesis** ('genesis'), **gigante** ('giant'), **general** ('general'), etc.

If a word derives from a basic one with **-j**, **–jo** or **–ja**, the **j** is retained: **espejeo (espejo), consejero (consejo), enrojecer (rojo), fijeza (fijo), granjero (granja), hojear (hoja), vejez (viejo)**, etc.

-Aje at the end of a word is a constant: **espionaje, garaje, sabotaje, lenguaje, paisaje, mensaje, porcentaje, salvaje, viaje.**[1]

There are only a few words where the letter **x** is pronounced as **jota:**[2]

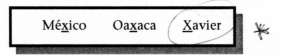

México	Oaxaca	Xavier

The sound of **g** as in **gustar** is spelled **gu-** before **-e** and **-i**, but is just **g** before **-a, -o,** and **-u:**

[1] There are very few exceptions, for example **colage** (Fren. and Engl. 'collage'), which retains the French **-g-**.

[2] A note about spelling: some people—not Mexicans—like to spell México with a **j** instead of an **x**. Mexicans know how to spell the name of their country—look at stamps and currency from that country to see how it is spelled.

guerra	Guillermo	ganar	gol	gusano

If a [w] sound is needed before **-e** or **-i**, you need to use a **u** with dieresis (**ü**); **gua** is pronounced [gwa]; **guo** is pronounced [gwo]:

[gwe, gwi]	güecho	argüir
[gwa, gwo]	Guatemala	antiguo

B and V

These two letters are pronounced exactly the same way, like the Spanish **b**, in the same phonetic circumstances.

It is easy to tell which letter to use a lot of the time because there are so many COGNATES[3] between English and Spanish which use the same consonant, and there are many words you already know how to spell. The problem words are, then, the uncommon words that are not cognates:

COGNATES:

visión, bisonte **búlgaro, vulgar**

WORDS YOU ALREADY KNOW:

vez, beso **ave, abeja**

LESS COMMON, NON-COGNATES (PROBLEM WORDS):

badajo 'clapper of a bell', **vajilla** 'dishes'

[3] A cognate is a word that looks and means about the same in two languages.

S, Z, C, X

The sound [s], as in **sing**, has four different spellings in Spanish. The letter **s** is pronounced as the basic English **s** before any vowel. In Latin America, **c** + **e,i** and **z** + **a,o,u,** are pronounced **s** as well. At the end of words, **-z** is also pronounced **-s:**

S BEFORE ANY VOWEL:

sacerdote, seco, sincero, sobre, sustituir

C+ E,I; Z+ A,O,U:

cine, cena; zona, azul, zambra

FINAL Z:

lápiz, avestruz

X + CONSONANT:

expirar, extremo, Taxco, explicar, extremo.

X can be pronounced **s** only before a consonant. This pronunciation is optional—you can pronounce **expirar** either "**ekspirar**" or "**espirar**" (but **Taxco,** the Mexican city, is always pronounced as if the **x** were an **s**).

H

H is never pronounced, so you have to know if one is present in order to spell it: of course, cognates again help out, as do words you already know:[4]

[4] The conjugation of **oler** uses an **-h** before **u**: **oler, huele**. This is because in medieval spelling **u** was used both for and **b** and **v**, so in medieval spelling, **uele** could be misread as **vele**. By putting an **h** before it, it could only be read [wéle] since **h** never preceded a **v**.

WORDS YOU HAVE TO KNOW:

Oaxaca vs. **almohada** | **oler** vs. **Holanda**
ilusión vs. **hilandera** | **amor** vs. **hamburguesa**

COGNATES AND WORDS YOU ALREADY KNOW:

honor, hora, hotel, hispano
haber, hoy, hasta

C, QU, K

The sound [k] is spelled **c + a,o,u** and **qu + e,i:**

C + A, O, U:	**casa, columna, culebra**
QU + E, I:	**queso, química**

U is never pronounced in the cluster **qu: qué, quizá.** But it is always pronounced following **c: cuento, cuanto.** There are just a few words unavoidably spelled with **k: kilómetro, Kremlin.**

EXERCISES

1. Fill in the missing letter that stands for the [x] sound, and write the English equivalent next to the word. (You may have to look up some of the words in the dictionary.)

el __apón	__oven
__enerar dinero	el __enitivo
__enético	__udicial
__eométrico	aconse__ar
el espiona__e	ad__etivo
__erusalén	ba__ar

el cora___e
de___ar
yo de__é de __ugar
el porcenta___e
el ___ardín
el ___emelo
el ___énero
el ___énesis
el ___igante
el ___udaísmo
el ___ueves
el aprendiza___e
el gara___e
el lengua___e
la mon___a

el pasa___e
empu___ar
en ___eneral
la ___ente
la ___itana
la ___oya
la ___ungla
la ___usticia
la venta___a
Mé___ico
aconse__ar
¡Aconsé___eme!
salva___e

2. Fill in the missing letter(s) for the [g] sound.

La _____allina pone huevos, el ___allo no.
La Se___unda _____erra Mundial terminó en 1945.
El entre___a su informe sobre ___oya.
La _____errilla Sendero Luminoso existió en Perú.
La _____inea Ecuatorial es un país en Africa.
La _____arantía caduca en un mes.
El meren_____e es un baile típico de la República Dominicana.
Me duele la ___ar_____anta.
En Europa hay muchos alber_____es juveniles.
La _____itarra es un instrumento de música.

3. Fill in the missing letter(s) for the [k] sound, and write the English equivalent next to the word:

el ___ilo	el bos___e
ad___irir	la es___ina
a___ello	el ___ilómetro
ar___eológi___o	___ími___o
al___ilar	la ta___illa
el ata___e	el papri___a
blan___o	___ebrar
a___í	el ___as___o
el ___eso	tran___ilo
el blo___e	me___áni___o
___alifi___ar	in___ai___o
es___iar	vol___áni___o

4. Fill in the missing letter(s) for the [s] sound.

¿Vamos ___in o con Juan?

¿Es ___imple o difí___il?

Yo soy un hombre ___in___ero, de donde cre__e la palma.

¿Quién no cono__e la La ___infonía nº 9 de Beethoven?

Treinta y __inco (35) y veinti__inco (25) son ___e___enta (60).

La ___e___e___ión o separación definitiva de Portugal de España ocurre en 1640.

Contemos: ___ero, uno, do___, tre___, cuatro, ___inco, ___eis, ___iete, die___, on___e, do___e, tre___e, cator___e, quin___e, die___iseis,...

¡Luchemos por la pa___ en el mundo!

los Amish son pa___ifistas.

La capital de Vene___uela es Caraca___.

El oxígeno es un ga___.

La capa___idad de esta sala es ___incuenta per___onas

Vivimos en el segundo pi___o de la ca___a.

Tienes que ven___er la pere___a si quieres sacar buenas nota___.

Sui___a y Sue___ia son dos paí__es europos.

5. Is there an **h** in these words?

Este muchacho es capaz de ___acer el trabajo porque es muy ___ábil.

El pobre niño es ___uérfano.

El ___acero es un metal.

John ___abla español.

Mira ___acia la derecha.

Una ___acacia es un árbol o ___arbusto de flores ___olorosas.

El pan se hace con ___arina y ___agua.

Giuliani fue un ___alcalde muy conocido de Nueva York.

Ya no puedo más. Estoy ___arto de tus ___istorias.

Un ___istmo es una lengua de tierra que une dos continentes o una península con un continente.

___ay un ___ueco en la blusa.

Las gallinas ponen ___uevos.

El perfume ___uele muy bien.

No quiero ___oler su perfume.

Hay muchos ___indúes en la India.

¿Qué ___ora es a___ora?

¡___ojalá venga Juan!

4

Consonants, the Phonetic Alphabet, and Phonemes

Consonants and Vowels

You learned in grade school that the vowels are **a, e, i, o,** and **u** (and sometimes **y**), and that all the other letters represent consonants. But no one ever defined what the difference between the two was. The difference is very clear: a vowel is a sound that comes out of your mouth with nothing getting in the way. When you say *ah!* or *ee!* or any other vowel sound in any language, it flows out of your mouth unimpeded. A consonant, on the other hand, is a sound that has some impediment that squeezes, stops, or reroutes the sound before it leaves your mouth.

The next several lessons are going to deal with Spanish consonants—how to produce them, and how they contrast with English consonants; and suggestions for overcoming stumbling blocks caused by interference from English consonants when you are pronouncing Spanish. Before you begin this study you need to know three things in order to explain (or understand) how a consonant is produced: 1) if it is VOICED or UNVOICED (Spanish: SORDO and SONORO) 2) where it is articulated, 3) how it is articulated.

First, you need to know whether the consonant is voiced or unvoiced (also called VOICELESS). If you put your finger on your voice box when you produce the sound of **m** or **v**, you'll feel the vibrations of your vocal cords because those two sounds are voiced. When you produce the sounds of **f** or **sh** with your finger in the same place, you'll feel no vibrations, because those sounds are unvoiced. The **p** of **pin** is the unvoiced version of the **b** of **bin**. The **s** of **phase** is the voiced equivalent of the **c** in **face.**

The second thing you need to know is the consonant's POINT OF ARTICULATION (Spanish: PUNTO DE ARTICULACIÓN)— which is where the sound is produced. **M, p,** and **b** are all articulated between your lips. They are all BILABIAL[9] sounds. Your two lips close completely when you produce **m**, and the resulting sound comes out of your nose; the **p** and **b** are sounds that are initially stopped between your lips and then are released, the first one being voiceless and the second one voiced.

LABIO-DENTAL consonants are articulated with your lower lip at your upper teeth. **F** and **v** are labio-dental sounds.

INTERDENTAL sounds are produced when you put your tongue between your teeth. English has two: the **th** of **bath** and **bathe**.

Just behind your teeth is the **alveolar ridge**. You can feel with your tongue that just behind this ridge the roof of your mouth slopes up rather steeply. Consonants articulated with your tongue at your alveolar ridge are logically called ALVEOLAR [pronounced "alveelur" in English]. **S, z, t, n, l,** and **d** in English are all alveolar sounds: **see, zebra, tin, now, low, din.**

PALATAL sounds are made with your tongue at the roof of your mouth. The **sh** of **ash** and the **s** of **pleasure** are palatal consonants.

VELAR consonants are articulated with your tongue at the back of your mouth. The **k,** the **g** of **go,** and the **ng** of **king** are velar consonants.

Spanish adds DENTAL consonants to this list. In Spanish, **t** and **d** are dental.

The third thing you need to know is how the consonant is produced, its MANNER OF ARTICULATION (Spanish: MODO DE ARTICULACIÓN). A number of consonants are in some way constricted or squeezed before they leave your mouth. These are called FRICATIVES (Spanish: FRICATIVO).

The **s** of **see**, the **f** of **free**, the **s** of **pleasure** are fricatives because the sounds are constricted. There are several fricatives in English, and a few more in Spanish.

An OCCLUSIVE (Spanish: OCLUSIVO) is a sound which is completely stopped then released. The **p** of **pin**, the **t** of **tin** and the **k** of **kin** are unvoiced occlusives; the **b** and **g** of **big**, and the **d** of **din** are voiced occlusives. There are several occlusives in English and Spanish.

NASAL (Spanish: NASAL) consonants are also stopped in your mouth with your tongue or lips, but they exit through your nose. The **m** of

---

[9] All of the names for points of articulation are spelled the same way in English and Spanish.

more, the **n** of **nor** and the **ng** of **sing** are nasal consonants. Spanish has these three and adds three more.

The last three categories are important but have few members.

An AFFRICATE (Spanish: AFRICADO) is a combinations of occlusives and fricatives. The **ch** of **chin** is an affricate—it starts out as an occlusive and ends as a fricative.

LATERALS (Spanish: LATERAL) are consonants that are produced at the sides of your mouth and include the **l** sounds of **love** and **hall.**

The FLAP and the TRILL (Spanish: VIBRANTE SENCILLO and VIBRANTE MÚLTIPLE) have those names because they are produced by flapping your tongue off the alveolar ridge. The Spanish **r** in **caro** is a flap, and the **rr** of **carro** is a trill. American English **rs** are neither flaps nor trills, although the same sound as the Spanish **r** of **caro** does exist in English, but it's not spelled **r.**

Once you know these three reference points, you can describe virtually any consonant, whether it exists in English or not, and the person you describe it to—knowing the same three concepts—should be able to produce it. So, if you say that the **g** of **hago** in Spanish is a "voiced velar fricative" your friend should be able to reproduce it. If your French friend can't seem to pronounce the initial **th** of **think** (that sound doesn't exist in French)—he or she may say **sink, fink** or **zinc** instead—all you need to do is say: "No, no, don't you see? It's an unvoiced interdental fricative!" And that should do the trick—maybe—if that person knows these phonetic definitions. The problem is that the sound is new to that person, and old habits are tough to break; new habits are tough to acquire. Bear this in mind if your progress seems slow in this course.

THE PHONETIC ALPHABET

In the mid-1880s, some British scholars at Cambridge University organized the International Phonetics Association. They realized that every letter of the Roman alphabet could represent several different sounds, not only in English, but within the range of world languages. They wanted to invent a set of symbols each one of which would represent a single discrete speech sound and would be valid for any language.

Here are some problems that are easily overcome with the phonetic alphabet. Within English itself there are enormous variations. Compare, for example, the **-ng-** sounds of **singer, finger,** and **ginger.** Or compare the **g** sounds of these pairs, which show only minimal differences in

Modo de Art.
fricativo africado
oclusivo lateral
nasal vibrante sencillo, múltiple

spelling: **forger, forget; anger, danger; eager, wager; laughter, daughter.** Examine the three different ways double **s** is pronounced in **possession** and **assign.**

Look at how **who-** is pronounced in **who, whole,** and **whoa.** Look even at the **-s-** in **house** and **houses.** Pronounce the difference between **should** and **shoulder.** And here are five different pronunciations of **-ough-: rough, trough, through, thorough, thought.** Here are three ways to pronounce the combination **-ear-: hear, heard, heart,** and three ways to pronounce **-omb: bomb, comb, tomb.** And how about the **-ove** of **move, love,** and **dove** (the past tense of **dive**)? the three letters of **ice** aren't always pronounced that way: look at **police, justice, licorice.** See if you can pronounce these words in two different ways each: **wound, produce, refuse, polish, lead, present, object, invalid, row, does, sewer, sow, wind, number, tear, subject.** Look at how you pronounce **graduate** in these two examples: "I'll **graduate** in June, then I'll be a **graduate** student." The spelling of a word in English simply doesn't indicate its pronunciation accurately, and in order to read aloud, you need to know how the word is pronounced.

Among foreign languages, the problem is compounded. **Ch** in English and Spanish is pronounced the same way (**channel, chiste**). But in French and Portuguese, it's always like the **sh** of **ship** (Fr. **cache**, Ptg. **chave**); in Polish it's like the Spanish *jota* (**chór** = chorus); in Italian it's like a **k: chianti.** The **ç** is like double **s** in French and Portuguese, but in Turkish it's like the English **ch (çok** 'very').

A major problem exists when a speaker of one language tries to pronounce something in a foreign language, and naturally uses the sounds associated in his or her *own* language, not having any idea of the patterns of letters seen in the foreign words. What else can you do? If you are at the ticket window of the train station in Warsaw and you want to go to **Łódź**, and if you say: "Lodz!" (kind of like "loads," as English speakers might say it) no one will understand you because the name of that city is pronounced "woodj" (as in "*Wouldy*a like a soft drink?"). There was an American girl in Madrid who was trying to get to the Plaza del Callao and stopped someone and asked: "Callao?" (Where she pronounced **-llao** as in "*layo*ver"). Needless to say, she was not understood. Pronouncing words in a foreign language using the sound patterns of your own is what is known as being GRAPH-BOUND.

Given the dizzying array of pronunciations for a single letter, and the vast number of possible speech sounds in the world's languages, these British philologists came up with the International Phonetic

Alphabet. They kept the letters of the Roman alphabet (each one designating one specific speech sound) and invented about twenty-five variations of these letters and a series of about thirty diacritical marks (accents are diacritical marks) to serve various purposes.

If our travelers had had phonetic transcriptions of the places they were looking for, [wǘʒ] (for Łódź) and [kayáw] (for Callao), they would have been perfectly understood.

You'll learn the Spanish letters of the phonetic alphabet (and some English ones, too) as you move through the book.

FAMILIES OF SOUNDS

Being graph-bound is a major, and very natural and even unavoidable, stumbling block, but an even more serious problem deals with "families of sounds." Every language has its own set of families of sounds. A family of sounds is a series of sounds, more or less related phonetically, each one being used in a different phonetic circumstance. Native speakers of a language are typically unaware that there is any variation at all among these sounds. Look at the English **t**. The **t** family has several variations. At the beginning of a word (and at the beginning of a stressed syllable), the **t** is accompanied by a puff of air which is strong enough to blow out a match, even when you whisper it: **tick**, for example. If it is the second sound in a syllable, it is pronounced with no puff of air: **stick**, for example (if you blow out a match when you shout **stick** it may be due to the hissing of the **s** and not to the **t**). Normally a **t** is articulated so that your tongue first shuts off the flow of air at your alveolar ridge, then releases it; but at the end of a word, a **t** doesn't have to be released, as in **bat**. In words where a **t** precedes an **l**, the **t** is released laterally, as in **bottle**. In American English, the **t** between vowels is typically flapped, as in **get up**! That makes five variations of the same sound. If you use the same sound, the **t** of **tick**, all the time, and don't use any of these variations, you'll be perfectly understood (although some people might think your pronunciation is odd—which it would be) because you will have stayed within the same family of sounds. All this seems obvious enough so far.

How can you tell one family from another? If you substitute another sound and the word means the same thing (as was suggested with the **t**s), it's from the same family. If you substitute another sound and the word means something different, it's from another family. In English we have three little families of sounds, one for the **n**, one for the **m**, and another for the **ng** of **sing**. In English, **seen, seem** and **sing** mean three *different* things, therefore those nasal sounds are members of three different families. Again, pretty obvious still.

In Spanish, an **n** assimilates to—it moves to the same point of articulation as—the following consonant. The word **sin** is pronounced "seen" in **sin dinero;** it is pronounced "seem" in **sin bases;** and "sing" in **sin ganas.** Those three sounds are members of the *same* family in Spanish because the three variations all mean the same thing: *without.* You can see where a problem arises when a Spanish speaker is trying to learn English and applies the rules of the Spanish "**n** family" (which he or she'll do unconsciously, as second nature) to English "I have seen dogs" (OK so far), "I have seem bananas" (uh, oh!) And "I have sing cats" (what does *that* mean?).

When you apply the sound families of English to Spanish, you have an "American accent." Once you know the sound families for both languages and how they work, you can start using the Spanish sound families correctly and be on the road to pronouncing Spanish like native speakers do.

Linguists don't call these "families of sounds," they call them PHONEMES. We'll call them phonemes, too, from now on. Phonemes are identified by characters placed in between slashes, for example /n/ means "the phoneme **n.**" The members of the family are the sounds themselves. They are represented by phonetic characters between brackets, [n], for example. Sounds between brackets—members of phonemes—are called ALLOPHONES. Phonemes are names, not sounds. Since they represent a family of *different* sounds they themselves have no phonetic value. The concept is easy to grasp if you think of people, the Marx Brothers, for instance. The family name is between slashes, /Marx/. The individuals are [Groucho], [Harpo], [Chico], [Zeppo], and [Gummo]. You can say: "Draw me a picture of [Chico]," because he is an entity with face and form, but you cannot say: "Draw me a picture of /Marx/," because Marx is just a name which represents five quite different individuals. Another example: /General Motors/. You can't say: "Well, I think I'll go buy a /General Motors/," because that's the name of the company that produces vehicles from tiny cars to giant tractors. You have to say: "Well, I think I'll go buy a [Cadillac]." What could be potentially confusing is that the *same* symbol is frequently used for the phoneme and one of its allophones, /n/ and [n], for example. Just tell yourself: "A phoneme is just a name, and the allophones are the sounds themselves. A phoneme doesn't represent any specific sound."

In this book, we will describe each phoneme in this way: first we'll

Familia = fonemas (are names not sounds)

give the name of the phoneme between slashes, and then we'll list the allophones individually, between brackets. Each consonantal allophone is then described by saying if it is voiced or not, where it is articulated, and how. And we'll also list in what phonetic environment it is found.[10] This is much less confusing than it may appear here, as you'll find out when you see the next lesson. You'll see that some phonemes have only one allophone and some phonemes have several. One Spanish phoneme has six allophones.

---

[10] Phonetic environments are basically these. Let's use **k** as an example: initial position (**cat**), between vowels [that is, INTERVOCALIC] (**accord**), final position (**rack**), between a vowel and a consonant (**recluse**), between a consonant and vowel (**alcohol**), between consonants (**banks**). Sometimes the environments will be very specific, such as between a vowel and a certain consonant.

5
Phonemes /p, t, k/

WHAT COULD BE SIMPLER—you might say—than to begin with these *easy* sounds? But the Spanish [p, t, k] are likely to take you a very long time to master. The problem isn't that you'll be graph-bound, since the sounds are similar. You don't have to say: "Hm, there's a **t.** I wonder what sound it *really* stands for." The problem lies in the interference caused by the English phonemes. Here are the Spanish phonemes with their descriptions and phonetic environments:

/p/		
	[p]	unvoiced bilabial occlusive, without aspiration, in all environments (except final): **pensar, esperar, aplauso, capa**
/t/		
	[t̪]	unvoiced dental occlusive, without aspiration, in all environments (except final): **tal, estrella, hasta, criticar**
/k/		
	[k]	unvoiced velar occlusive, without aspiration, in all environments (except final): **calor, asco, accidente, aquí**

Notice that these sounds are pronounced the same way in every allowable phonetic environment. Observe as well that the **t** in Spanish is dental that is, pronounced with your tongue just at the top of your upper teeth. Now compare the Spanish phonemes with the English phonemes, and you'll see that if you use the English phonemes for Spanish words, you'll create a few problems:

/p/		
	[pʰ]	unvoiced bilabial occlusive, with aspiration, in initial position, and beginning a stressed syllable: **pit, peck, impeccable**
	[p]	unvoiced bilabial occlusive, with no aspiration in all other environments: **spit, speck, happy, lap, aspiration, caps**
/t/		
	[tʰ]	unvoiced alveolar occlusive, with aspiration in initial position, and beginning a stressed syllable: **tick, tall, attract**
	[ɾ]	voiced alveolar flap between vowels, spelled **t** or **tt: later; better; I gotta go; get up, get outta bed**
	[t]	unvoiced alveolar occlusive, without aspiration in all other environments: **stick, stall, heat, hats, lasting**
/k/		
	[kʰ]	unvoiced velar occlusive, with aspiration in initial position, and beginning a stressed syllable: **cat, kin, incredible**
	[k]	unvoiced velar occlusive, without aspiration in all other environments: **skat, skin, seeking, track, lacks, asking**

You can easily see where the interference lies. If you apply the English phonemes to Spanish, initial **ptk** will be aspirated at the beginning of words; in intervocalic position, **t** and **tt** will be pronounced [ɾ], exactly like the Spanish **r**, between vowels; and (of lesser importance) the English alveolar **t** will be used instead of the Spanish dental **t.**[1]

---

[1] The Spanish dental **t** (and in the next lesson the dental **d**) may easily be the most difficult sounds to master for English speakers since the difference between an unaspirated dental **t** and an unaspirated alveolar **t** is subtle. But if you perfect all Spanish sounds but these, it's likely no one will ever notice your imperfect **t**s and **d**s.

Here are some easy ways to overcome these problems.

Avoiding aspiration isn't as hard as it might seem. English **pit, tick,** and **cat** have aspirated sounds in initial position, but if you change them into words with initial **s**, they are *never* aspirated: **spit, stick** and **scat.** So, if you do exercises in Spanish where the **ptk** aren't in initial position and gradually work around to where they are, you can fool your organs of speech into producing the Spanish sounds correctly. For example, if you chain together the name **Oscar** many times and change it into **caros**, you can fool your speech organs: **OscarOscarOscar OscarOscaroscaroscaroscaroscaroscaroscaros.** You can try the same with **costar/ tarcos** and **aspar/ paras** for **t** and **p**.

Another way of trying to eliminate aspiration is to consider that initial **ptks** are **bdgs**, since the voiced versions are never aspirated. Start out with initial **bdg** then unvoice them to **ptk**. For example, say **basta** ten times or so, then change it to **pasta** and see if that can fool your speech organs. We have exercises like this below.

The problem with the English **t** between vowels is not difficult to fix if you are aware of it. When you say **pato** ('duck') you don't want it to come out **paro** ('work stoppage')

Through being aware of the problem you can also change the English alveolar **t** into a Spanish dental **t.**

EXERCISES

Phoneme /p/

1. After an **s**, **p** is not aspirated in English, unless it begins a stressed syllable. Repeat the list of words below where the **p** begins an unstressed syllable:

caspa	esperar	obispo	áspero
césped	chispas	huésped	obispos
áspero	desesperado	diáspora	disparar
disponer	disputar	esperar	español
espiral	hospital	perspicaz	próspero

2. Now repeat these words where the **p** begins a word, following an **s**, but still in an unstressed syllable. If you pronounce them as if the article plus the word were a single word, you should be able to avoid the aspiration.

lospedazos	los pedazos	laspelículas	las películas
laspajadas	las pajadas	lospilotos	los pilotos
lospacientes	los pacientes	lospimientos	los pimientos
lospadrinos	los padrinos	laspiñatas	las piñatas
laspaellas	las paellas	lospoderes	los poderes
lospaisajes	los paisajes	lospoemas	los policías
laspalabras	las palabras	lospolicías	los policías
lospeinados	los peinados	lospulmones	los pulmones
laspreguntas	las preguntas		
lospeligros	los peligros		

3. An initial **b** in English is not aspirated but an initial **p** is. In this exercise you should try to fool your speech organs. First repeat each word in the first columns several times in a row (**babel/babel/babel...**), and then repeat the word in the second column several times in a row (**papel/papel/papel...**) concentrating on the non-aspirated **b** sound when you produce the **p**.

baja	paja	beca	peca
bajada	pajada	besar	pesar
bala	pala	beso	peso
banda	panda	boca	poca
baño	paño	bollo	pollo
bar	par	bomba	pompa
basa	pasa	borra	porra
basto	pasto	bote	pote
bata	pata		

4. Now read these maxims.

Al buen pagador no le duelen prendas.
La perdiz por el pico se pierde.
Palos porque bogas, palos porque no bogas.
Perdiendo aprendí: más vale lo que aprendí que lo que perdí.
El que mucho abarca poco aprieta.
El que compra barato compra cada rato.

Phoneme /t/

5. After an **s**, **t** is not aspirated in English, unless it begins a stressed sylable. Repeat the list of words below where the **t** begins a non-stressed syllable:

esta	estadística	estación	estatura
estimular	estudiar	castellano	castigar
costa	destacar	destilería	distinción
fiesta	festival	gasto	gusto
hasta	justo	lástima	místico

6. Now repeat these words where the **t** begins a word, following an **s**, but still not in a stressed syllable.

lostambores	los tambores	lastenazas	las tenazas
lostabacos	los tabacos	lostobillos	los tobillos
lostaburetes	los taburetes	lostoledanos	los toledanos
lostalentos	los talentos	lostomates	los tomates
losteatros	los teatros	lastonterías	las tonterías
losteclados	los teclados	lastormentas	las tormentas
lostecnólogos	los tecnólogos	losturistas	los turistas
lostejidos	los tejidos	lostucanes	los tucanes
losteléfonos	los teléfonos	lasturbinas	las turbinas
lostemores	los temores	losturrones	los turrones

7. Repeat each word in the first columns several times in a row (**dejado/dejado/dejado...**), and then repeat the word in the second column several times in a row (**tejado/tejado/tejado...**) concentrating on the non-aspirated **d** sound when you produce the t.

dan	tan	dejo	tejo
dango	tango	dele	tele
dardo	tardo	denso	tenso
data	tata	día	tía
daza	taza	doce	tose
debajo	te bajo	Dora	tora
debate	te bate	domar	tomar
deja	teja	danto	tanto
dejador	tejador	dos	tos
deje	teje	duna	tuna

8. Before a **u**, **t** is frequently pronounced **ch** as in **chin** or **sh** as in **shin** in English, but just a dental **t** in Spanish. Read the following pairs of English and Spanish words (that don't always have the same meaning):

ENGLISH	SPANISH	ENGLISH	SPANISH
adventure	aventura	mutual	mutuo
conceptual	conceptual	natural	natural
eventual	eventual	overture	obertura
cultural	cultural	ritual	ritual
habitual	habitual	textual	textual
intelectual	intelectual	virtual	virtual
lecturer	lectura	actual	actual

9. Now read the following maxims.

A los tontos no les dura el dinero.
Tanto monta, monta tanto.
Tanto tienes, tanto vales; nada tienes, nada vales.
El que temprano se moja, tiempo tiene de secarse.

Phoneme /k/

10. After an **s**, **k** is not aspirated in English, unless it begins a stressed syllable. Repeat the list of words below where the **k** begins a non-stressed syllable:

asco	escalar	escalera	escasez
buscador	búsqueda	máscara	músculo
pescador	emboscada	mayúscula	minúscula
rascacielos	casco	exquisito	fresco
bosque	morisco	mariscos	quiosco

11. Now repeat these words where the **k** begins a word, following an **s**, but still not in a stressed syllable.

loscamarones	los camarones	lascabezas	las cabezas
losqueridos	los queridos	lascabinas	las cabinas
losquetzales	los quetzales	loscobijos	los cobijos
loskilómetros	los kilómetros	loscocineros	los cocineros
losquioscos	los quioscos	loscocodrilos	los cocodrilos
lascamisas	las camisas	loscochinos	los cochinos
loscaimanes	los caimanes	loscuadernos	los cuadernos
loscaballos	los caballos	loscubiertos	los cubiertos
lascabañas	las cabañas	loscuchillos	los cuchillos
loscabellos	los cabellos	lasculebras	las culebras

12. Repeat each word in the first columns several times in a row (**galgo/galgo/galgo...**), then repeat the word in the second column several times in a row (**calco/calco/calco...**) concentrating on the non-aspirated **g** sound when you produce the **k**.

galo	calo	gata	cata
gacha	cacha	gato	cato
gacho	cacho	gaucho	caucho
gala	cala	gayo	cayo
gallo	callo	godo	codo
gama	cama	gola	cola
gano	cano	goda	coda
gasa	casa	goma	coma
gasta	casta	gorra	corra
gasto	casto	gorro	corro

13. Now read the following maxims.
Adonde el corazón se inclina, el pie camina.
A quien Dios quiere para si, poco tiempo lo tiene aquí.
Cortesía de boca mucho consigue y nada cuesta.
De cuerdo y loco todos tenemos un poco.
El casado casa quiere.
En casa de carpintero, puerta de cuero.
Mal que no tiene cura, quererlo curar es locura.
El que tiene boca se equivoca.

FINAL EXERCISE

14. These sentences were taken from various newspaper articles, and each one has several **p, t, k** sounds in different phonetic environments.

a. Le faltó sorpresa y se quedó a mitad de camino entre la propuesta y la actitud.

b. El fiscal reconstruyó las últimas horas de Axel, desde que intentó escaparse de la casilla donde estaba cautivo.

c. Los policías antisecuestros cordobeses tenían ubicado el lugar y se disponían a actuar.

d. El Gobierno inició conversaciones para alcanzar un acuerdo bilateral y se trataría de favorecer la llegada de productos argentinos.

e. Los tres detenidos fueron trasladados en un avión de la Gobernación, desde el Aeropuerto Córdoba.

f. Mil quinientos efectivos están destinados a la custodia y no pueden ocuparse del patrullaje callejero.

g. Gaudí fue un referente para Dalí, tanto en su obra como en sus escritos. Lo valora mucho como arquitecto y por su sentimiento católico.

h. La pedrera, el Park Güell y la Sagrada Familia son los ejes centrales del recorrido y en torno a los cuales se estructuran los dibujos, pinturas y documentos.

i. La estructura ideada por el presidente y ejecutada a pies juntillas por Jorge Valdano, también en entredicho, ha caído del altar por el peso de problemas futbolísticos y por una actitud de soberbia y exceso de confianza que ha terminado por pasar factura.

j. El futuro Ministro de Economía español se encontrará cuando tome posesión con unas cifras de crecimiento superiores a la media comunitaria.

6
Phonemes /b,d,g/

THIS SERIES OF PHONEMES has two sounds that we don't have in English, but if you produce and get accustomed to them as described, you shouldn't have problems. You already know that Spanish **b** and **v** are pronounced exactly the same way.

/b/
- [b] voiced bilabial occlusive
  - after silence: **¡Bueno! ¡Victoria!**
  - following a nasal: **un burro, un vaso, hambre, envío**
- [β] voiced bilabial fricative
  - between a non-nasal consonant and a vowel: **árbol, calvo**
  - all other environments (except final): **fabuloso; llevar; fiebre, obligación; alba, Cervantes**

/d/
- [d̪] voiced dental occlusive
  - after silence: **¡Despiértense!**
  - following a nasal: **andar, un diputado**
  - following l: **caldo, aldea, el dorado**
- [ð] voiced interdental fricative
  - between vowels: **hada, odontología**
  - between a vowel and a consonant: **padre, cuadro**
  - between a consonant $^{(-\text{nasal}, -\text{l})}$ and a vowel: **ardiente, desde**
  - final position: **calidad, cantidad, entrad**

/g/
- [g] voiced velar occlusive
  - after silence: **¡Gracias a Dios!**
  - following a nasal: **un gato, tengo**
- [ɣ] voiced velar fricative
  - between a vowel and a consonant: **vinagre**
  - between a non-nasal consonant and **a, o, u**: **órgano, algo, arguye**
  - between any vowel and **a, o** and **u**: **hago**

Basically the same phonetic environments affect all three phonemes the same way, except that the **d** remains occlusive after **l**, whereas the others don't. English does have the sound [ð], but it is spelled **th** as in **leather.** English doesn't have [β] or [ɣ]. The Spanish [d̪] is dental but the English [d] is alveolar. Also, note that the Spanish fricative **d** exists in final position whereas the others don't.

Here are the English phonemes:

/b/
- [b] voiced bilabial occlusive
  in all positions: **bless, fabulous, gab, cabriolet, obliterate**

/d/
- [d] voiced alveolar occlusive
  in all positions except between vowels: **dear, hard, bedridden**
- [ɾ] voiced single alveolar flap
  between vowels: **adage, ladder, I've had it!**

/g/
- [g] voiced velar occlusive
  in all positions: **go, bag, agriculture, argon, sagging**

The same [ɾ] sound of **t** or **tt** between vowels in English also affects the **d** or **dd.** The English [d] is alveolar as was the [t]. It is important to be aware of the interference of the English **d, dd** between vowels and to practice the fricative allophones in Spanish.

EXERCISES

Phoneme /b/

1. A **v** after silence is always pronounced [b]:

Victoria	vicaria	víctima	vid
vídeo	vidrio	vidente	vil
villano	voz	vosotros	vocero
vaso	vasco	vascular	vuelo
vuelta	vulgar	vecina	veinte

2. The same goes for **v** after **n**; therefore the **nv** of **con vos** sounds like the **mb** of **hombre.** Pronounce the **v** after **n** in the following words:

circunvolar	con Valerio	con Víctor	convalecer
convencer	conversar	convertir	convivir
convocar	el convento	el envase	el invernadero
el tranvía	en Valencia	en vano	sin vacaciones
enviar	invadir	envejecer	gran ventaja

3. Pronounce the **b** in the following examples as [β]:

débito	debe	doble	debate
debajo	débil	noble	tobillo
tobillo	bobo	cobarde	sabe
Alberto	álbum	abandonar	habitual
habitante	cable	gabinete	cubano

4. Pronounce the following pairs of words.

cave	cueva
salvation	salvación
cavern	caverna
save	salvar
savage	salvaje
avid	ávido
David	David
my victory	mi victoria
... and vice versa	... y viceversa
the position is vacant	el puesto está vacante
to be on vacation	estar de vacaciones
He is very vicious.	Él es muy vicioso.
the vice president	el vice-presidente
She is a vegetarian.	Ella es vegetariana.
She is very vindictive.	Ella es muy vengativa.

5. Do you pronounce **v/b** as [b] or [β] in the following newspaper headlines?

A. DETENIDO EN VALENCIA UN PRESUNTO ETARRA QUE PREPARABA ATENTADOS EN LEVANTE PARA ESTE VERANO

B. UN PERRO SALVA A UN VAGABUNDO POR UN MENSAJE EN UNA BOTELLA

C. CONDENADO A PAGAR DOSCIENTOS VEINTE EUROS A UN VECINO POR VIOLAR SU INTIMIDAD AL COLOCAR UNA CÁMARA PARA VIGILAR A SUS INQUILINOS

D. EL AVISO DE UN VECINO CONDUCE A LA APREHENSIÓN DE CUATRO MIL KILOGRAMOS DE COCAÍNA EN VALENCIA

Phoneme /d/

6. Pronounce the **d** in the following words as dental occlusives:

dama	Dante	dañar	dar
dato	debajo	decano	decente
dando	candela	andar	aldea
Andalucía	Andrés	Andorra	caldera
balde	molde	onda	banda

7. Pronounce the **d** in the following examples like the English **th** as in **that**, but shorter:

barbudo	leído	idéntico	comodidad
credibilidad	fidelidad	idealidad	identidad
modalidad	adversidad	solidaridad	productividad
adeudado	estadidad	variedad	acomodado
adecuado	adoptado	graduado	radioactividad

8. Pronounce the following words and decide whether the **ds** are pronounced [d] or [ð]:

fundado	candado	cordialidad	debilidad
densidad	dignidad	diversidad	indignidad
defendido	demanda	difundir	clandestinidad
frondosidad	grandiosidad	profundidad	

Phoneme /g/

9. Read the following words and decide whether the **g** should be pronounced [g] or [ɣ]:

Angola	agave	ingrato	mongol
agobiar	pedagogo	congruente	conglomerado
congratular	sinagoga	agregar	vanguardia
gigante	demagoga	Góngora	segregación
agregar	ganga	Augsburgo	gringo
Galápagos	Gregorio	garganta	congregación
pedagoga	gallego	ángulo	griego
	segregar		abrigo

10. These sentences were taken from various newspaper articles, and each one has several of the **g** sounds in different phonetic environments.

a. El profesor Pérez fue llevado ante el intendente municipal de la ciudad de Buenos Aires, Manuel Güiraldes, quien, poco después, lo designó laringólogo honorario del Teatro Colón que aún no se había inaugurado.

b. José Caminal explicó que en el organigrama del Liceu, como en otros teatros europeos, no figura el cargo de jefe de seguridad.

c. Desde el punto de vista del administrador, un buen organigrama es el que facilita el trabajo y un mal organigrama, el que lo dificulta.

d. ¡Seguro que lo has visto al Maera! El más sangregorda y el más tranquilo en el mundo entero.

e. La empresa, creada por el grupo Ercrós tras la segregación de Explosivos Río Tinto, podría verse obligada a cerrar definitivamente su segmento de producciones militares.

f. El padre Viganó ha sido un auténtico maestro y guía de la congregación en estos años de renovación y de cambio.

g. En plena campaña para la elección del Parlamento gallego, Fraga reiteraba en una entrevista que "empecinarse en mantener el referéndum es una gran equivocación." Aseguraba que dicho error debía "pagarlo el Gobierno de su bolsillo" y condicionaba "pedir que se vote" a la formulación de una pregunta "que no cierre el futuro" y no suponga la aprobación de la política exterior gubernamental.[2]

h. Tras una serie de averiguaciones policiales se supo la fecha y el lugar de llegada de un yate gallego que iba a desembarcar en la isla un importante cargamento de droga.

i. Y Celia pudo comprobarlo durante la ocupación del pueblo, cuando un muchacho gallego anunció en la plaza de la parroquia que deseaba abandonar la guerrilla, que no aguantaba más.

j. Un catalán o un gallego podrían pertenecer a ISOC España.

FINAL EXERCISE:

11. These sentences were taken from various newspaper articles, and each one has several of the **b**, **d**, **g** sounds in different phonetic environments.

a. Además, una ofensiva creíble para la pacificación y la modernización de estos países debe ir de la mano de un diálogo.

b. Las democracias tienen la obligación de demostrar mediante sus actos, que realmente son democracias.

c. Fue trasladado a un hospital, pero no tiene ninguna herida de

[2] The audio program for this exercise goes only this far.

gravedad.

d. Dada la necesidad de consultas y de discusiones adicionales con los acreedores, es difícil establecer un preciso cronograma para lanzar y completar la oferta.

e. Debemos salir de esta reunión con decisiones.

f. "La mala educación" es la decimoquinta película de Pedro Almodóvar.[3]

g. Saint-Exupéry desapareció después de partir de la isla de Córcega a bordo de su avión para una misión de reconocimiento destinada a preparar el desembarco aliado en Provenza.

h. Con la suficiente velocidad, un vehículo espacial puede liberarse de la gravedad terrestre y entrar en una órbita alrededor del Sol, como la de un planeta.

i. El cava y el champán son dos vinos espumosos de gran personalidad. Se distinguen por su linaje y estilo, el suelo donde arraigan las vides, las uvas que los producen y el método de elaboración. Todo ello les aporta..., el tamaño de la burbuja y su expresión aromática.

j. La excavación más grande llevada a cabo desde 1986, es la de Bet Sheán. Se han revelado partes considerables de la ciudad romana, que estuvo poblada también en el período bizantino y el árabe antiguo. Paralelamente, los arqueólogos volvieron a excavar en la antigua colina donde se levantaba la ciudad en la Edad de Bronce.

---

[3] The audio program for this exercise goes only this far.

7
Phoneme /s/

THE [s] AND [z] SOUNDS IN Spanish are members of the same phoneme in Spanish, but in English they are members of two different phonemes.

/s/

[s] unvoiced alveolar fricative
- in word-initial position: **seña, zona, cerca**
- between vowels: **caso, mazo, acerca**
- after any consonant: **absoluto, adscrito, alzar consonante, comienzo**
- before any unvoiced consonant: **hasta, caspa, asco, esfera, gazpacho, explicar**
- in final position: **todas, avestruz**

[z] voiced alveolar fricative
- before any voiced consonant: **desde, Lisboa, rasgo, asno, chisme, portazgo**

It is true that sometimes speakers will say **mismo** and **asno** with [s] instead [z], and this is perfectly all right since they are still using the same phoneme. But it is practically impossible to keep the [s] before **d** as in **desde**.

An **s** typically disappears before **r: la~~s~~ ramas** [larámas], **I~~s~~rael** [iraél], **má~~s~~ redondo** vs. **mar redondo** [mareðóndo], **de~~s~~ramar** vs. **derramar** [deramáɾ]. There is nothing either substandard or dialectal about this. It's hard or impossible to pronounce the cluster otherwise. This will be further treated in the next leason, which deals with **r**.

The sound [s] is spelled **s** + *any vowel* and **z** + *any vowel* and both in final position: **sábado, secular, siniestro, soler, supremo, carros;**

Zamora, zócalo, cazuela; crisis, libros, avestruz, actriz. It is also spelled **c + e,i** in Latin American Spanish: **hace, cimiento.** Optionally, as you remember from Lesson 3, an **x** + consonant can be pronounced [s]: **experiencia, extra.** There is nothing substandard in this pronunciation either, although many educated speakers choose to pronounce it [ks] before a consonant: **expirar, extensión.** The allophone [z] is spelled s or z: **desde, capataz‿bueno.**

In English there are two phonemes, /s/ and /z/, a fact that is easily proven by the pairs, **face** and **phase; rice** and **rise.** Phonetically there are no problems for English speakers since both languages have the same sounds. But English speakers have to be careful when they pronounce intervocalic **s** in Spanish since they pronounce it [z] as in English: **present** vs. **presente; resident** vs. **residente.**

Also, while it's true that English speakers sometimes pronounce **s** before a voiced consonant as [z], as in **husband** and **mesmerize**, many times an **s** before a voiced consonant is pronounced [s], as in **busboy, disband.** Finally, English speakers, seeing a **z** in Spanish frequently become graph-bound and pronounce them erroneously [z] in such words as **Zamora, raza.**

EXERCISES

1. The letter **c** before **e** and **i** is pronounced like [s]. Read the following words:

acepción	adolescencia	concepto
complacencia	concepción	creencia
decepción	docencia	excepción
inocencia	licencia	percepción
recepción	Cicerón	ejercicio
piececitas	superficie	obcecación

2. Pronounce the following pairs of words in English and Spanish. Remember that in Spanish the **s** and the **z** (Latin America) in these contexts are always voiceless:

ENGLISH	SPANISH	ENGLISH	SPANISH
basilica	basílica	resolve	resolver
Caesar	César	result	resultado
phase	fase	rose	rosa
physically	físicamente	visit	visita
music	música	zenith	cenit
nasal	nasal	zinc	cinc
reserve	reserva	Zodiac	Zodiaco
resident	residente	zebra	cebra
residue	residuo	zone	zona
resignation	resignación	Byzantine	bizantino
resist	resistir	base	base

3. Which of the following **s** and **z** are voiced?

cacicazgo
comadrazgo
compadrazgo
desdecir
desdén
desdicho
durazno
esdrújula
hallazgo
juzgar
liderazgo
lloviznar
noviazgo

sin rasgo
muchos daños graves
les debo dinero
los dejo aquí
las damas danesas
los días del año
Esto nos dice mucho
son las diez de la noche
son las doce del día
las dotes de mando
los dos duros de Juan
las dudas de María

4. The letter x in the following examples can be pronounced [s] (or [ks]).

extra
mixto
textiles
excarcelar
excavar

exceder
excelencia
excéntrico
excepcional
excitación

exclamar	exportar
excluir	sexto lugar
extrovertido	texto
inexcusable	extinción
inexperiencia	externo

5. The letters **s** or **ss** followed by **u** or **i** in English are sometimes pronounced [ʒ] or [ʃ] (= "sh"), but in Spanish it's always [s]. Say the following pairs of words:

<u>ENGLISH</u>	<u>SPANISH</u>	<u>ENGLISH</u>	<u>SPANISH</u>
visual	visual	magnesia	magnesia
usual	usual	pleasure	placer
casual	casual	lesion	lesión
treasure	tesoro	fissure	fisura
Asia	Asia	mission	misión
Indonesia	Indonesia	vision	visión

6. Read the following sentences:

a. Creo que la experiencia de la infancia es muy superior a la de la adolescencia.
b. Las veintitrés piececitas de este registro, breves, sencillas, inspiradas y honestamente andalucistas, revelan a un músico que supo encontrar su sitio.
c. La nueva línea se ha diseñado para una velocidad máxima de trescientos km/h, con excepción de varias restricciones a doscientos cuarenta km/h en algunos tramos de curvas existentes en Módena.
d. La auténtica oposición ha sido físicamente destruida en los famosos procesos que han esmaltado el régimen de Hassan II, en las ejecuciones y las persecuciones como consecuencia de los complots y, en caso necesario, con truculencias como el asesinato de Ben Barka en París.
e. El canciller hondureño Delmer Panting dijo a periodistas de su país que las fuerzas de seguridad de Honduras, desplegadas en la zona fronteriza con El Salvador, tienen orden de capturar a los salvadoreños que talen el bosque ilegalmente.

8

Phonemes /ɾ/ and /r/

ONE OF THE GREAT giveaways that a person is a native speaker of American English is the use of the American **r** instead of the Spanish **r.** The American **r** has no phonetic equivalent in any European language, so it is difficult for foreigners to master, not only for its uniqueness, but for other reasons which will be explained—but not in this lesson.

You have already seen the Spanish [ɾ] sound represented by the English **t, tt, d,** or **dd** between vowels and you already pronounce it perfectly since it exists in English. You just have to get used to its new spelling as **r.** You will also have to get used to the spelling using phonetic letters.

/ɾ/

[ɾ] voiced alveolar flap

between vowels: **caro** (always written with one **r**)
following a consonant (not **l, n, s**): **abre, acre, agrio**
preceding a consonant (not alveolar or dental, except for [s]): **cargo, marchar, cárcel, arde**
final position: **singular** (= free variation)

/r/

[r] voiced alveolar trill

between vowels: **carro**
word-initial position: **mi rosa, la rama**
following **l, n, s: alrededor, honra, Israel**
preceeding a dental or alveolar consonant (not [s]): **arte, pierna, Carlos**
final position final: **singular** (= free variation)

FREE VARIATION means that either sound can be used.

The only place where these two phonemes contrast is between vowels: **caro** vs. **carro**; **ahora** vs. **ahorra**.

Regarding the [r], how long should your trill last? ±3 seems appropriate.

Students are often surprised to learn that all **r**'s that begin words *always* use the trilled **r**, but it is so.

EXERCISES

1. Read the following series of words. If you replace the **r** mentally with an English **d**, you should be able to pronounce the Spanish [ɾ] correctly.

práctica	practicable	practicante
pradeña	pradera	pradejón
precario	precariamente	precariedad
preceder	precedente	precedencia
precioso	preciosa	preciosamente
pregunta	preguntar	preguntador
premio	premiar	premiación
prenda	prender	prendido
prensa	prensar	prensado
prueba	probar	aprobado

2. Pronounce the following pairs of English and Spanish words. The Spanish r sounds exactly like the English **t**, **tt**, **d** or **dd** in **later**, **better get up**, **ladder**, **header**.

caro	baro	cara	pirineo
lera	hierba	era	erizo
lempira	llorar	barba	barco
perilla	extra	pero	Ebro
obra	piedra	África	comprar
otro	agrio	Carmen	largo
ofrenda	aprieto	Ucrania	abrir

3. Trill the initial **r** in the following words. Don't pronounce the **s** in the articles in the plural examples.

la rabia	las rabias	el roble	los robles
el rabo	los rabos	el robo	los robos
la ración	las raciones	la roca	las rocas
el radar	los radares	el rocío	los rocíos
la raíz	las raíces	el rodeo	los rodeos
el rallo	los rallos	el ron	los rones
la rama	las ramas	la ropa	las ropas
la rana	las ranas	la rosa	las rosas
el rancho	los ranchos	la rosca	las roscas
el rango	los rangos	el rubí	los rubíes
la rebaja	las rebajas	la rueda	las ruedas
la red	las redes	el ruido	los ruidos
el riesgo	los riesgos	la ruina	las ruinas
el rigor	los rigores	la rumba	las rumbas
la rima	las rimas	el rumbo	los rumbos
el río	los ríos	el rumor	los rumores
la risa	las risas	la runa	las runas
el rival	los rivales	la ruta	las rutas

4. Read across. Pronounce the [ɾ] in the first word of the series, and then the [r] in the following three words.

abrir	aburrir	aburre	burro
escaparate	parte	aparte	arte
probamos	borla	borrar	borroso
cráter	carril	Carlos	Carlota
cruel	corral	corta	corla
groso	gorro	ahorro	aorta
aparato	parto	esparto	harto
parado	porto	comparto	ortopedia
poroto	pierna	aporto	perrera
perenal		perla	

5. Pronounce the [ɾ] and the [r] in the following pairs of words:

ahora	ahorra	mira	mirra
buró	burro	moro	morro
caro	carro	para	parra
cero	cerro	paro	parro
coro	corro	pera	perra
ere	erre	poro	porro
foro	forro	cura	curra
hiero	hierro	toro	torre
hora	horra	turón	turrón

6. Read the following tongue-twister:

Erre con erre, cigarro;
erre con erre, barril;
rápido ruedan los carros cargados del ferrocarril.

7. Read the following sentences taken from various Spanish newspapers.

a. El amplificador pertenecía a otro radiorreceptor mucho más grande que el que posee.
b. Ese viaje fue su reencuentro con el Perú profundo y el primero de una serie interminable que lo llevó a recorrer el país de cabo a rabo.
c. Los autores explican que "la inexistencia de fuentes escritas que hagan referencia específica a la vida de los ferroviarios ha hecho necesario recurrir a las fuentes orales, y más concretamente a entrevistas realizadas a los trabajadores que han desarrollado la totalidad de su vida profesional en RENFE [= *Red Nacional de Ferrocarriles Españoles*].
c. Ante el poder económico del frente Domingo Laín y la rebeldía de varios frentes en cinco regiones de Colombia, el cura Pérez aceptó reestructurar el ELN (*Ejército de Liberación Nacional*) y tratar de conjurar una división al interior de la organización.
d. En Cuba, se considera que el consumo de los refrigeradores puede representar entre 30 y 50 % del consumo en el sector residencial.
e. En la práctica, lo que el Ministerio de Ciencia y Tecnología, en coordinación con el área de Universidades del Ministerio de Educación, está tratando de hacer es liquidar a muy corto plazo el programa Ramón y Cajal, y aprovechar la "flexibilidad" de la también controvertida Ley Orgánica de Universidades, de la que

faltan por desarrollar múltiples decretos, entre ellos, el del profesorado, para "tratar de reincorporar a los Ramón y Cajal como son los contratos para doctores investigadores," coinciden el rector y el representante de esta sección.

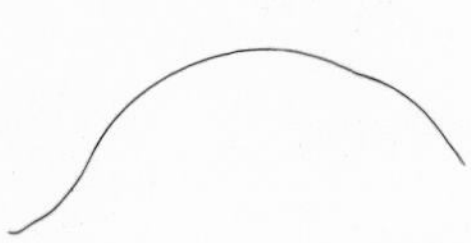

9

Phonemes /m,n,ñ/

THE PHONEME /m/ IS pretty straightforward, with only one allophone [m]. The letter **m** always represents the phoneme /m/.

The phoneme /n/ has *six* allophones—more than any other Spanish phoneme—because /n/ will assimilate to the point of articulation of the following consonant.

The phoneme /ñ/ has only one allophone. Here are the nasal phonemes in Spanish:

/m/

[m] voiced bilabial nasal
  word initial: **¡Mamá!**
  between vowels: **amo, imitar**
  before [p,b]: **lámpara, ámbar, invitar**

/n/

[n] voiced alveolar nasal
  word initial: **¡Nunca!**
  between vowels: **Anita, cana, uranio**
  before an alveorlar consonant: **cansado, cómanlo, honra**
  end of word before silence (or before an alveolar consonant): **¡No hablen! con redes**

[ɱ] voiced labio-dental nasal
  before **f**: **énfasis, enfermo, un fuego**

[n̪] voiced dental nasal, before **t, d**: **anda, antes**

[ɲ] voiced palatal nasal, before [č]: **ancho, un chico**

[ŋ] voiced velar nasal
  before [k,g] and the *jota* sound: **ancla, tengo, ángel**

~~[m] voiced bilabial nasal~~
  ~~word final **n** before [b,p]: **un burro, un puro, un vaso**~~

/ñ/

[ɲy] voiced palatal nasal followed by [y]

The notion that [m] is an allophone of /n/ seems innocent enough, but the laws of phonemics state that a single sound, such as [m], can belong to only *one* phoneme. Well, here [m] belongs to two different phonemes: /m/ and /n/. Some linguistics will go to enormous lengths to make this thorny problem come out right (and we won't go into what they do here). Maybe they're right. We're just trying to be practical.

What makes the combination [ɲy] a phoneme unto itself is that there is a contrasting pair of words that careful speakers differentiate: **huraño** (*shy like a rabbit*) and **uranio** (*uranium*).

Note that [ŋ] is used within words before [x]: angel [áŋxɛl], but not between words: un juego [un xwéɣo].

Here are the three English nasal phonemes:

English

/m/		
	[m]	voiced bilabial nasal in all positions: **me, comet, lamp, alms, dumb, some comet, some trick, some bat**
	[ɱ]	voiced labio-dental nasal the letter **m** before [f] within a word: **emphasis, camphor**
/n/		
	[n]	voiced alveolar nasal in all positions: **neat, any, ant, ethnic, beaten, seen bats, seen tulips, seen cats**
/ŋ/		
	[ŋ]	voiced velar nasal in all positions, except initial: **anger, singer, youngster, ping, sing better, sing dreamily,**

The allophones of the English nasals are members of three different phonemes, but in Spanish the same four sounds belong to the *same* phoneme /n/.

English speakers have easy-to-overcome problems with Spanish:

1) [ŋ] belongs to the family /n/ in Spanish but belongs to the /ŋ/

family in English.

2) There is no /ñ/ phoneme in English.
3) Nasals don't assimilate to following consonants in English (except for the labio-dental **m** in words like **emphasis**, and an **n** assimilates to a **k** or **g** inside words like **anchor** and **anger**). Also, there is no assimilation in: **I have seen dogs, seen cats, seen burros.**

EXERCISES

Phoneme /n/

1. Repeat these examples with **mp. Compilar** (to *compile*) and **con Pilar** (*with Pilar*) sound exactly alike. Read across the page.

combate	con bata
compacientes	con pacientes
compadecer la desgracia	con padecer la desgracia
compadre Ambrosio	con padre Ambrosio
comparar los coches	con parar los coches
comparte la casa	con parte de la casa
compasión	con pasión
compatriotas	con patriotas
complacer	con placer
compresa	con presa

2. **Nv** is also pronounced [mb]. **Con vino** sounds like **combino**, and **en vías** like **envías.** Repeat these lists:

convencer	convención	convencional	convenio
convenir	convento	convergencia	conversar
envase	enviar	envolver	invadir
inválido	invasión	inventar	invento
un vago	con validez	con valor	sin vino

n m conmigo
n m inmenso

3. The **n** in Spanish **énfasis** is pronounced [ɱ] as in English **emphasis**. Pronounce the following words:

confección	conflicto	conforme	confuso
enfermo	enfermera	enfadar	enfático
enfrentar	enfriar	infancia	infarto
infectar	infeliz	inferior	infinito
influencia	informe	infusion	ninfa

4. Now pronounce the same cluster between words:

en forma	con factura	con facilidad	con falda
caer en falta	sin falta	en familia	un fantasma
un faro	con fiebre	con fecha	un film
un filósofo	sin fin	con flan	un filete
en Florencia	un fósforo	en Francia	con Félix

5. The **n** before [č] is pronounced [ɲ]. Read the following words.

chico	un chico	chico	un chico
champú	un champú	chicano	un chicano
chaval	un chaval	chino	un chino
checo	un checo	chile	un chile
cheque	un cheque	chiste	un chiste

6. Before [k], [g] and [x], within words, the **n** in Spanish is pronounced [ŋ] such as in the English **finger**. Read the following pairs of words to hear and note the difference between [n] and [ŋ].

Ana	ancla	tenor	tengo
anular	angular	vena	venga
cono	Congo	viene	vengo
canela	Ángela	vino	vínculo
mono	hongo	mina	ingenio

7. The same applies to **n** at the end of one word and the sounds [k] and [g] at the beginning of the next word if there is no pause between them.

un gato	en Guinea	sin grifo
un gran guía	un globo	Carmen grita
con ganas	cien godos	con gusto
han ganado	un golpe	sin cambio
tienen ganas	con gorro	un café
con gas	sin gozar	han caído
sin gas	cien gramos	sin cambio
han gastado	sin grasa	con cobre
un gasto	con gripe	con cloro

8. Repeat these sets of words with dental **t** and then with dental **nt**.

ata	anda	padre	panda
beta	venda	pedir	pendiente
bota	bondad	pido	pinto
cada	anda	sede	sentir
cata	canta	SIDA	sintagma
codo	onda	sido	siento
cuota	contra	tata	tanta
dedo	dentro	Tito	tinto
mata	manda	zeta	centro
mido	miento		

Phoneme /ñ/

9. Prounce the following pairs or words and pay attention to the different pronunciation of –**nio**- and –**ño**-.

amonio	moño	geranio	extraño
anión	año	junio	puño
Antonio	otoño	helenio	beleño
arsenio	señorito	opinión	cañón
convenio	huelveño	unión	el Peñón
demonio	rascamoño	vulcanio	castaño

10. Read the following text about Felipe II's military architect, being careful to pronounce all the allophones of /n/ correctly.

JUAN BAUTISTA ANTONELLI: ARQUITECTO DE LAS DEFENSAS DE FELIPE SEGUNDO EN VARIOS PAÍSES DE AMÉRICA

¿También te fascinan los corsarios o los piratas del Caribe? El siguiente texto es sobre un arquitecto militar que dedicó su vida para repeler a los piratas de los principales puertos españoles alrededor del Caribe en el siglo dieciséis y diecisiete.

A finales del siglo dieciséis incursiones de los corsarios franceses, ingleses y holandeses convencieron al rey Felipe Segundo de encargar a Juan Bautista Antonelli que realizara mejoras en las defensas de su imperio. En esta época, los conflictos con Francia se habían intensificado y las cordiales relaciones con Inglaterra habían comenzado a deteriorarse aunque la media hermana de la reina Isabel de Inglaterra se había casado con Felipe. La reina Isabel aprobó el comercio ilegal, promoviendo así la carrera de corsarios ingleses, cuyas incursiones en el Caribe son tan famosas. La actividad de los corsarios era una empresa conjunta respaldada por los inversionistas ingleses y la nobleza. Todos compartieron las ganancias de un viaje exitoso. De esta forma, muchos centros españoles de riqueza y transporte en América, eran presa de un creciente número de corsarios.

Los reyes de España conocieron bien a la familia Antonelli. Era una dinastía de ingenieros civiles y militares que ya habían diseñado defensas e instrumentos de asedio en Rusia y Hungría contra las invasiones de los otomanos. También Juan Bautista se había convertido en un destacado profesional. La primera misión encomendada a Antonelli fue la fortificación del estrecho de Magallanes, pero por razones que probablemente nunca se sabrán, el capitán general Diego Flores de Valdés, comandante de la expedición, saboteó la expedición. El ingeniero tuvo suerte de regresar con vida a España. Los buenos oficios de un amigo impidieron que el nombre de Antonelli se viera envuelto en el desastre del estrecho, asegurándole un nuevo encargo real. Aunque debilitado por problemas de salud y frecuentes conflictos con funcionarios coloniales, esta nueva misión inició la fase culminante de su carrera como arquitecto militar.[4]

Primero fue a Cartagena, la ciudad que había vivido muchos años de conflictos con los piratas. Antonelli diseñó un plan para aprovechar la capacidad defensiva del lugar. Le pareció obvio que el bloqueo y la fortificación de las entradas naturalmente angostas de la bahía resultarían mucho más eficaces para impedir una invasión que los terraplenes tan fácilmente superados por Drake. Sus asistentes también construyeron fuertes temporarios y se iniciaron los trabajos de un plan permanente de defensa con tres masivas fortalezas.

Antonelli también pasó tiempo en Cuba y en Panamá. En mil quinientos ochenta y ocho el rey le encomendó convertir los planes de defensa de Cartagena en piedra y argamasa.

En mil seiscientos dieciséis, la muerte terminó su odisea de cuarenta años al servicio del rey.

(Adaptation of: "Arquitecto de las defensas del rey." *Américas*, Octubre, 2003, pp. 6-15.)

FINAL EXERCISE:

11. Read these selections from various newspaper articles.

a. Respecto a la situación de la tercera edad, una población cada vez más numerosa, Alberdi cree que a pesar de la proliferación de residencias para ancianos en todas las comunidades autónomas, nuestros mayores desean estar cerca de los suyos.
b. El enemigo, por consiguiente, es caricaturizado hasta el punto de considerarlo el más malintencionado de los enemigos imaginables.
c. Los diez mandamientos son para cumplirlos, independientemente de si se tiene un ángel de la guarda al lado que le este diciendo que hay que cumplirlos.
d. Y teniendo en cuenta que la situación económica no sólo es manifiestamente mala en las regiones, sino dentro de la propia Rusia, el problema podría ser más grave de lo que parece.
e. La financiación de la Iglesia es uno de los temas que más preocupan a los obispos españoles, que desde el pasado mes de septiembre están manteniendo conversaciones con el Gobierno para conseguir

[4] The recorded portion in the audio program goes only this far.

una financiación estable.[5]

f. En la operación en zonas de mantenimiento y como mecanismo de emergencia, es posible operar los trenes en el modo manual a bordo del vehículo.

g. En este sentido, es significativo el nombramiento de los cuarenta y un senadores nombrados por el Rey, que casi pueden seguir siendo considerados como "de Ayete."

h. ...porque cada máquina, cada equipo, cada producto que importábamos subía de precio, mientras el precio de nuestro azúcar, principal renglón exportable, que era el del mercado mundial, más una prima de preferencia y el de otros productos básicos, se mantenían fijos a partir de los precios alcanzados el primer año del convenio.

i. Por supuesto que, en su tiempo, se cometieron muchos abusos por las fuerzas de seguridad pero la mayoría de víctimas eran delincuentes comunes y éstos se mantenían bajo control.

j. Los nombres que se mencionan para conformar la Comisión de la Verdad son de gente muy honorable, pero la comunidad médica está escandalizada porque alguien quiere colar a un médico que no ha pagado un préstamo con COFINA y nunca dio explicaciones sobre el uso de material médico propiedad del Estado en su clínica privada.

[5] The recorded portion in the audio program goes only this far.

10
Phoneme /l/

THE PHONEME /l/ IN Spanish is quite different from the /l/ phoneme in English.

/l/

- [l] voiced alveolar lateral, used in all positions, except before dental and palatal consonants: **lejos, ala, costal, alma, Carlos.**
- [l̪] voiced dental lateral, used only before [t̪] and [d̪]: **alto, caldo.**
- [ʎ] voiced palatal lateral only before [č]: **el chico, colchón.**

English has only two variations.

/l/

- [l] voiced alveolar lateral.
  - word initial position: **lunch, let's**
  - between vowels: **calendar, mallet**
  - after a consonant: **flight, pleasure, glass**
- [ʟ] voiced velar lateral
  - before a consonant: **colder, alphabet, calcium, falls**
  - in word-final position: **hall, smell**

The allophone /ʟ/—which is just fine in English—sounds awful in Spanish. The English phonemic pattern wants to interfere before consonants and in word-final position in Spanish. You will have to pay special attention and work hard to get used to the Spanish patterns.

EXERCISES

1. Pronounce the following series of words, and try to pronounce the **l** in the last word (with the l in final position) like the **l** in the two words before. Read across the columns.

alalá	ala	al
Elena	ele	el
pelele	pelea	piel
sola	ola	sol
colilla	cola	col
Liliana	lila	mil
ensalada	sale	sal

2. Pronounce the **l** in the second column the same way as in the first one.

calamar	calma	lanzar	alcanzar
alabar	alba	Lázaro	alcázar
alegre	álgebra	culinario	culminación
hola	Olga	colina	culmina
balón	balcón	olor	olmo
alejar	almejar	colo	colmo
balena	almena	escalo	calmo
ala	alma	palo	palmo
ala	alba	alea	aldea
ala	alca	calor	caldo

3. Read the following tongue twisters with the letter **l**.

Qué col colosal colocó en aquel local el loco aquel.
Qué colosal col colocó el loco aquél en aquel local.

Pablito clavó un clavito ¿qué clavito clavó Pablito? Cabral clavó un clavo ¿qué clavo clavó Cabral?

La piel del jovial Manuel, siempre fiel a la ley local, luce como la miel de un panal singular.

FINAL EXERCISE:

4. The following sentences were taken from various newspaper articles. Read them and pay attention to the pronunciation of /l/.

a. **Cocaleros bloquean carretera boliviana**

Unos cinco mil cocaleros protagonizaron un bloqueo de la principal ruta de Bolivia, en contra de la proyectada instalación de tres bases militares en la convulsa región del Chapare. Los productores comenzaron el bloqueo de la vía que vincula el eje troncal del país conformado por los departamentos de La Paz (oeste), Cochabamba (centro) y Santa Cruz (este).

b. **Dañan reloj solar en la ciudadela incaica de Machu Picchu en el Cuzco**

La estructura pétrea conocida como Intihuatana o reloj solar, en la célebre ciudadela incaica Machu Picchu, resultó dañada al caerle encima el brazo de una grúa mecánica, durante el rodaje de un comercial de televisión... Su deterioro causó indignación en círculos intelectuales y culturales, que cuestionan la falta de un reglamento especial para proteger el parque arqueológico de Machu Picchu, que es Patrimonio Cultural de la Humanidad.

c. **Argentina propone al tango como patrimonio de la Humanidad**

El gobierno argentino lanzó en la UNESCO la candidatura de Tango como patrimonio oral e intangible de la Humanidad. La presentación consistió en un trabajo de investigación con material producido por las academias nacionales de tango de Argentina y Uruguay. El expediente contiene copias de partituras originales de temas famosos, libros de colecciones y un CD multimedia con música, biografías y películas.

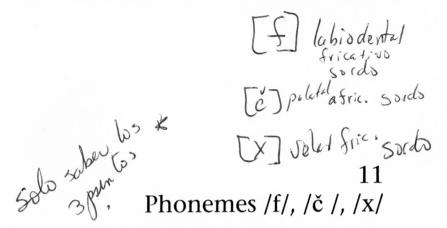

11

Phonemes /f/, /č /, /x/

THE FIRST TWO PHONEMES are easily recognizable. /f/ has one allophone, [f], and it's just like the English sound, an unvoiced labio-dental fricative. You need to know the phoneme, of course, but you don't need exercises. It's used in all positions except final in Spanish. In English the [f] sound is used in word final position, but never in native Spanish words. /č/ also has only one allophone [č], an unvoiced palatal affricate. It sounds just like the English [č], and it is used in all allowable positions— not before a consonant and not in final position. You don't need exercises for this sound either.

The phoneme /x/ has only one allophone, [x], an unvoiced velar fricative. The reason an **x** is used to represent this sound is that Greek and Russian use the letter **x** to represent it. The English **h** is officially an "unvoiced pharyngeal fricative," more like breathing out. The Spanish /x/, on the other hand, is rather strongly articulated.

/x/
[x] unvoiced velar fricative
all allowable positions; not before a consonant or in final postion: **jamón, ajo, enjambre, Gilberto, género, coger, México**

There are only a couple of Spanish words ending in **-j**, one of them being **reloj**. But that **-j** really is never pronounced until you make the plural **relojes**.

EXERCISES:

1. G before e and i is pronounced [x]. Read the following examples:

ángel	erigir	margen	gira
agitar	escoger	origen	gitano
acoger	exigir	página	Ángela
coger	fingir	surgir	región
colegio	frágil	virgen	rígido
elegir	gel	gemelo	ungido
elogio	Gil	género	vigilar
emergencia	imagen	genial	angina
energía	magia	gente	lógico

2. ¿[g] or [x]?

ligero	negligencia	granjero
geólogo	genético	jaguar
demagogia	regiones	jerga
gigante	agasajar	juego
geológico	agigantar	jugador
pedagogía	agregar	jugoso
gigantesco	aguajero	juzgado
agregar	agujero	lagartijo
geógrafa	ajeno	lenguaje
Georgia	anglosajón	mujeriego
ginecóloga	cangrejo	reciclaje
griego	granja	pasajero

3. The following sentences were taken from various newspaper articles. Read them and pay attention to the pronunciation of the letters **g** and **j**.

a. Aseguró que no hacía demagogia al señalar que "es paradójico que estas propuestas lingüísticas las proponga un partido que tiene en su seno a los representantes de las oligarquías que en su día expulsaron de su tierra a una gente que tuvo que venir a Cataluña a ganarse el pan.

b. Ahora lo lamentamos porque el supuesto tráfico o traslado ilegal de menores a Venezuela, refleja nuestra negligencia a todo nivel: policial, jurídica, socio-económica.
c. Primera novela del poeta Juan Bonilla, *Nadie conoce a nadie* (Ediciones B) es una extensa y ambiciosa obra que narra la engañosa y difícil relación de dos personajes obsesionados por la literatura. Al fondo, una compleja maquinaria terrorista convertida en un gigantesco juego de rol que alguien maneja a su antojo.
d. Un mes antes de que su padre abandonara el cargo, relajada y sonriente, con varios cambios de vestuario, Zulemita le dio un extenso reportaje a la revista *Caras*, su preferida. A Zulemita le fascinaba el estilo del semanario de *Perfil*. Fotos grandes y un lenguaje ligero. Amaba verse reflejada en sus páginas.

12

Vowels

SPANISH HAS ONLY SEVEN basic vowel sounds; American English has *at least fifteen.* On the one hand, the Spanish vocalic system is much less complex than the English system, and on the other, the phonemic system of American English gives ample opportunity for phonetic interference. If you use American vowels in Spanish, it makes Spanish utterances sound really awful. Don't get us wrong—American vowels are wonderful, but when substituting for Spanish vowels, they are responsible for the brunt of the American accent.

You learned in the previous chapters that you need three bits of information in order to define a consonant: 1) if it is voiced or voiceless, 2) its point of articulation, and 3) its manner of articulation. To describe vowels, you also need three bits of information, different from—and not as exact—as what you need for consonants.

Here are the three things you need to know to form vowels. First, you need to know if the vowel is articulated in the FRONT of your mouth, in the CENTER, or at the BACK (Spanish: ANTERIOR, CENTRAL, POSTERIOR) Second, you need to know how high in your mouth the vowel is articulated: HIGH, MID, or LOW (Spanish: ALTA, MEDIA, BAJA). And finally, you need to know the position of your lips: are they SPREAD (as in the **ee** of b**ee**t), are they in a NEUTRAL position, at rest (as when you say **ah**...) or are they ROUNDED (as in the **oo** of **soon**) (Spanish: ESTIRADA, NEUTRA, REDONDEADA)?

For example, in Spanish, the [a] of **casa** is a low, central, neutral vowel; the [e] of **pelo** is a middle, front, spread vowel; and the [u] of **uno** is a high, back, rounded vowel.

The middle vowels show a refinement. Are they OPEN (*not* opened) or CLOSE (not closed) (Spanish ABIERTO or CERRADO)? The first **o** of **color** is a close vowel; the second **o** is open. If you look at yourself in a mirror when you say these two vowels, you will see that your mouth is physically more closed when you articulate the first vowel, and more open when you say the second one. The notion of open and close will only affect **e** and **o** in Spanish.

TYPES OF VOCALIC SOUNDS

There are three types of vowel sounds. P URE VOWELS start and end the same way. All of the seven basic Spanish vowels are pure. A GLIDE or SEMI-VOWEL (Spanish SEMI-VOCAL)[1] is the [y] or [w] sounds that, when

V. Puras
Deslisada

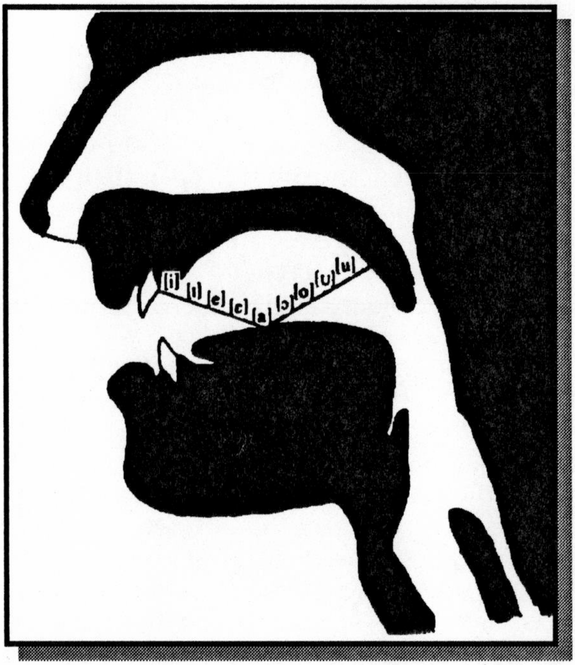

added to a pure vowel, make a diphthong (as in **hac*i*a**, **d*eu*da**) by gliding from one point of articulation to another. Glides can precede a pure vowel or come after it. That is, in **hac<u>ia</u>**, the diphthong starts high in the front of your mouth and glides immediately towards the **a**. In

[1]The **y** of **ay!** Is a semi-vowel because that sound moves up in you mouth; if it moves downwards, like the **y** of **ya** it is called a SEMI-CONSONANT. Let's have a gentleman's agreement to call *all* glides semi-vowels.

a baja central, labios centrales
u posterior alta, redondeados

deuda, the diphthong starts on the pure vowel **e**, then glides away to the upper back of your mouth. You already know that the third type of vowel sound, just mentioned, is a DIPHTHONG (Spanish DIPTONGO). Diphthongs are a combination of a glide—either preceding or following—and **a, e,** or **o.**

Spanish has seven pure vowel sounds, two glides, and any number of diphthongs.

SPANISH VOWEL PHONEMES

We'll treat the straightforward ones first: /i,a,u/:

/i/

[i] front, high, spread vowel
- in word initial position + a consonant: **istmo, invierno, hito, llama**
- between consonants: **dime, risa**
- in word-final position after a consonant: **corrí, maní, cursi**
- when stressed, anywhere: **hígado, frío, hacía, ríe**

[y] front, high, spread glide
- unstressed, in contact with **a, e, o: hacia, hielo, llama, yeso**
- between vowels {= **y, ll**]: **sello, playa.**

/a/

[a] central low neutral vowel
- in all environments: **alma, casa, llano**

/u/

[u] back, high, ~~rounded~~ redondeada vowel
- in word initial position + a consonant: **usted, uva, usado**
- between consonants: **atún, rústico, túnel**
- in word-final poisiton after a consonant: **Perú, espíritu,**
- when stressed, anywhere: **continúa, laúd**

[w] unstressed, in contact with another vowel: **deuda, continuo, cuidado, aula**

There is a further comment about the phoneme /i/. Instead of using the variant [y] between vowels, after **l** or **n**, or at the beginning of words, many speakers will use a softened [ǯ] (the **j** of **judge**): **sello** [se^{ǯ}o], **inyección** [in^{ǯ}eksyón], **yeso** [^{ǯ}éso]. The male Colombian speaker in the audio program seems to prefer [y] while the female Colombian speaker prefers [^{ǯ}] and In initial position a stronger [ǯ]. What does this mean for your pronunciation? Choose one version and perfect it.

a = neutral
e =

The phonemes /e/ and /o/ require you to know one more simple definition. These vowels will be variously open or close depending on if they are in an OPEN SYLLABLE or a CLOSED SYLLABLE (Spanish: SÍLABA ABIERTA, SÍLABA CERRADA). An open syllable simply ends in a vowel; a closed syllable ends in a consonant.

/e/

[e] front mid spread close vowel
- in an open syllable when not part of a diphthong: **hablé, Pepe, quepo, remo**
- the **e** of the diphthong **ie** in word-final position: **superficie, carie**
- in a final syllable closed by an **s**: **baile-bailes, pide–pides.**

[ɛ] front mid spread open vowel
- in a closed syllable: **lento, festivo, pestaña, doler, cuesta.**
- in an open syllable when followed by **r, rr**: **pero, ferrocarril, cera**
- the **e** of the diphthong **ie** (except in word-final position): **cielo,hiedra, bienestar**

These two allophones are very vexing at times, because different native speakers will pronounce an open **e** and others will pronounce a close **e** for the same word. Thus, some will say [kwɛ́sta] for **cuesta** and others [kwésta]. There is no phonemic difference, so you don't need to worry about changing meanings of words.

/o/

[o] back mid close rounded vowel

in an open syllable: **coco, amo, loquísimo**

in a syllable closed by [s] or by a nasal:

cósmico, los, caballos, onda, pomposo.

[ɔ] back mid rounded open vowel in any other closed syllable: **crisol, color**

A final note about Spanish vowels: They are all short and of the same length, so all syllables will take about the same amount of time to produce.

ENGLISH VOWELS

This list of vowels is guided by Hollywood pronunciation. There are six vowels that are diphthongs at all times, there are ten other vowels that are pure, and there are three glides.

The long vowels in English are mostly diphthongs. Most speakers diphthongize the **ee** of **seen** and the **oo** of **soon.** They are rather subtle diphthongs: ([íi, ʊ́u]). Look in the mirror when you pronounce those words and you will see that your lips move when you pronounce those vowels. If your lips move, even slightly when you say **ee** or **oo**, you are producing a diphthong. The other diphthongs are not as subtle, but they are absolutely unavoidable as anything other than diphthongs in English: [ey], [æy], [ay], [ow]. So, when Americans go to learn Spanish they naturally, unavoidably, pronounce **de** as [déy], and **hablo** as [áβlow] since they have no other way to pronounce the final **e** and **o.**

The diphthong [æy] is used only before [ŋ]: **bang, sang, dang!**

beet [íi]
bait [ey]
bang [æy]
bite [ay]
boat [ow]
boot [ʊ́u]

You'll have to work hard to eliminate the final glides caused by English interference. But how? Since the glide is always very short, and tacked onto the *end* of the diphthong, one thing you can do is pronounce the first part of the diphthong very long, something like [eeeeeeeeey]. Then pronounce it again, but chop it up into short pure vowels, putting the glide *only after the last one:* [e-e-e-e-e-e-e-e-ey]. Then, finally, stop short of the final glide the next time you say it: (e-e-e-e-e-e-e]. This same exercise works well with the interference caused by [ow]: [ooooooooow]; [o-o-o-o-o-o-o-o-ow], [o-o-o-o-o-o-o-o-o].

The next series is a set of pure vowels, some of them surprising.

bit [ɪ]
bet [ɛ]
bat [æ]
bot(tle) [a]
bore [ɔ]
but [ʌ]
bought [ô]
but(cher) [ʊ]
b<u>ur</u>n [r]
compl<u>i</u>mentary, duplic<u>a</u>te *(noun)*, phot<u>o</u>graph,
exc<u>e</u>llent, camp<u>u</u>s [ə]

The vowel [ɔ] is used only before the **r** sound.

The most surprising thing about the **ur** of **burn** is that the American **r** is really a *vowel* and not a consonant. The sound passes through your mouth without friction or interference of any kind—and that is what defines a vowel. For further proof, the British **er**, as in **father** (pronounced almost exactly like the first **a** in [fáðа], is decidedly a vowel). The Brooklynese **rs** in "I'll meet you goils at Toid Avenue and Toity Toid Street," are nothing but diphthongs, and since they are variant allophones of the same phoneme, all speakers of English understand that the girls should go to Third Avenue and Thirty Third Street. And when they refer to Cuba in Massachusetts and it comes out "Kyuber," they've substituted one vowel for another. So, here is a case of a vowel being spelled as a consonant. The use of American **r** in Spanish is another thing that sounds really dreadful, and is another giveaway that the speaker is American. What makes it difficult—even though we have the Spanish [ɾ] sound in English—is that it is hard for English speakers to change from their vocalic **r** to the consonantal **r** of Spanish. On the other hand, the American English **r** is a sound that is very tough for foreign speakers to master since there is no equivalent in any other European language.

The last vowel on the list, [ə], known as SCHWA, can have a very bad influence on Spanish pronunciation as well. In English, it replaces any vowel in most unstressed circumstances, as the examples in the box above show. Since each Spanish vowel is pronounced the same way whether stressed or not, it is very important to pay particular attention to the proper pronunciation of vowels. In English we pronounce Alabama [æləbǽmə] but in Spanish, there are four **a**'s pronounced the *same* way in **alababa** [alaβáβa].

There are three glides in American English.

[y] = y,i + vowel, vowel + i, y: **yellow, canyon**
[w] = u,w + vowel, vowel + w, u: **willow, cowboy**
[ɹ] = cons. + r, r + consonant: **free, cart**

There are so many vowels in English, you'd think that there would be a lot in common with Spanish vowels, but when you compare the two series of vowel symbols for both languages, you'll see that really only [ɛ], [ɔ], and [a] are shared between the two systems. Thus, English gives you pretty exact equivalents only for the Spanish vowels of **esto**, **por**, and **para.** The others will have to be worked on.

EXERCISES:

Phoneme /a/

1. Read the beginning of the **Balada para Amanda Argañaraz**, written by A. G. Corbella and published in the *Revista Tía Vicenta* (Buenos Aires), año VIII, número 281, mayo 1964, in which the author only uses the vowel **a**.

Acá van las palabras más francas para alabar a Amanda Argañaraz, alma arrastrada a la Nada tras la más malhadada batalla para alcanzar a amar al canalla más falaz; batalla parada tras larga zaranda para acabar abrazada a la Parca, arrastrada al mar.

¡Acallad las amargas palabras!

¡Paz para Amanda Argañaraz!

Amanda Argañaraz amaba la campaña: largaba las frazadas a la blanda cama al aclarar cada alba anaranjada.

Lavaba la cara, bajaba a la planta baja; para halagar a la mamá, cantaba raras baladas, tras sacar para yantar las tajadas más bastas a las manzanas, a las naranjas, a las bananas, a las granadas. Calzaba blancas alpargatas; calaba bata asargada, calzas batarazas, ancha faja, alba casaca, gabán calamar, pardas gafas. Apartaba la más mansa asna a la majada, atábala, cabalgábala, lanzaba la jaca alazana para vagar tras las cabañas más apartadas. Mas la dama jamás maltrataba la asna: Amanda amaba la jaca, tan mansa, tan llana, tan flaca...

2. There is also a text from the poet Rubén Darío, which only uses the vowel **a**. Read the beginning of this text.

Amar hasta fracasar

Faltaba ya nada para anclar; más la mar brava, lanza a la playa la fragata: la vara. Arranca tablas al tajamar; nada basta a salvar la fragata. ¡Ah, tantas almas lanzadas al mar, ya agarradas a tablas claman, ya nadan para ganar la playa! Blas nada para acá, para allá, para hallar a Ana, para salvarla. ¡Ah, tantas brazadas, tan gran afán para nada. Hállala, más la halla ya matada! ¡¡¡Matada!!!... Abraza a la amada: —¡Amar hasta fracasar!—clama...

3. Now read the following recipe, which has many occurrences of **a**.

Calabaza asada

INGREDIENTES:
1 libra de calabaza
6 cucharadas de leche
5 cucharadas de harina de
Castilla
3 huevos
1/8 libra de mantequilla
1 ramita de perejil
1 cucharadita de sal
1/8 cucharadita de pimienta

Preparación:

Se pela y se limpia de semillas la calabaza, cortándola en pedazos medianos. Se polvorean con pimienta molida, se rebozan y se fríen; se colocan en una cacerola plana o sartén grande. Se baten los huevos con la leche y la sal y se vierte sobre la calabaza. Se hornea durante media hora o se cocina en la olla de presión hasta que se ablande la calabaza. Se adorna con perejil, o si se prefiere con anillos de cebolla, tiras de ají pimiento asado o queso rallado.

4. Read this little children's rhyme.

CANCIÓN BRUJOSA

Brujas, brujitas y brujotas con brazos largos y medias rotas.
Abracadabra!
Patas de cabra!
Brotan embrujos en cada palabra.
Brujas sin dientes
¿Dónde estarán?
Si yo toco el timbre... ¿me abrirán?

5. Read the following Spanish palindromes.

Aman a Panamá
Ana, la tacaña catalana.
Atar a la rata.
Amad a la dama.
Ana lava lana.

Phoneme /e/

6. First, practice the close [e]:

beca	dejo	meta	seda
besa	ETA	neta	seta
beso	geta	pelo	tela
beta	jefa	peso	tema
ceja	jeta	peta	vega
cero	leña	rema	velo
dedo	letra	seca	veta

7. Final Spanish **e**s are especially troublesome because of the tendency of English speakers to pronounce them [ey]. Pronounce these words, being careful about the final **e**s:

abre	come	ere	Noé
aire	cree	ese	olé
arde	dame	fase	que
ave	debe	fue	ríe
base	efe	hace	trae
bebe	eje	lave	une
cae	ene	lee	uve

8. Read the following words and pronounce the **e**s either open (closed syllable) or close (open syllable).

eclesiásticamente	empequeñecer
efectivamente	empobrecerse
efervescencia	encendedor
ejecutivamente	encogerse
ejercerse	entender
electrónicamente	endurecerse
elementales	entremeses
emblemáticamente	entretener
embobecerse	equivalentemente
emergente	eternamente

9. Read the following Spanish palindromes.

Echele leche	Sé verle del revés
ser tres	Se es o no se es

Phoneme /i/

10. Read the following examples that all have stressed **i**s.

ahí	coquí	mambí
ají	di	Martí
así	esquí	mi
caí	frenesí	nací
alfonsí	iraní	rubí
aquí	iraquí	si
ceutí	israelí	ti
colibrí	jabalí	vi

11. Unstressed **i** next to any other vowel becomes the semi-vowel [y].

aliado	cielo	miocardio
aria	cien	miope
Asia	diez	boina
odiar	piel	coincide
triana	ceiba	estoico
baile	peine	oiga
fraile	reina	heroico
Cairo	seis	Celsius
gaita	veinte	ciudad
naipe	dio	triunfa
bien	dios	veintiuno
ciego	kiosko	viuda

12. Of course, the letter **y** is also pronounced [y], the same as the letter **ll.**

yacer	creyó	oye	silla
yate	cuyo	playa	brilla
yegua	ensayo	rayo	villa
yerba	fluye	reyes	valle
yo	Goya	llave	lleno
yoga	haya	llano	lloro
apoyo	huye	calle	lluvia
ayer	joya	bello	llanto
ayuda	leyó	gallo	ella
cayó	maya	sello	allá

Phoneme /o/

13. The biggest giveaway that you are an English speaker is pronouncing the Spanish **o** as [ow], especially stressed **o** at the end of syllables and words. This is very tempting for you because in English syllables and words rarely end in a stressed **o.** Here it is either followed by a consonant or one of the three glides. Try pronouncing the following words without a glide, as close, short **o**s.

no	mío	uso	cayó
yo	cojo	mosca	curó
ajo	loro	veo	bobo
amo	pozo	habló	como
amó	oyó	pensó	foro
año	los	miró	loco
asó	tío	leyó	robo
coco	ufo	bosque	rojo
dio	uno	bajó	roto

14. All of these Spanish words have [ɔ]

orca	forzar	fortuna	torre
borda	forca	norma	golpe
corneta	forma	bolsa	molde
dormir			

15. Read the following words and pronounce the **o**s either open (closed syllable) or close (open syllable).

octógono	odontóloga	odontología
odontológico	oligotrófico	onomasiológico
olopopo	oloroso	oncológico
oncólogo	onomatopéyico	ontológico
ontólogo	oponiéndolo	ornitológico
ortodoxo	osteológico	otorrinolaringólogo

16. Read the beginning of a song written by León Grieco that uses only the vowel **o**.

Ojo con los Orozco

(CORO): Nosotros no somos como los Orozco,
yo los conozco son ocho los monos:
Pocho, Toto, Cholo, Tom, Moncho, Rodolfo, Otto, Pololo.
Yo pongo los votos sólo por Rodolfo,
los otros son locos, yo los conozco,
no los soporto. ¡Stop! ¡Stop!
¡Pocho Orozco!

Odontólogo ortodoxo, doctor.
Como Bolocotó, oncólogo jodón.
Morocho, tordo, groncho, jocoso, trosco,
chocó con los montos. Colocó molotov.
¡Bonzo!
¡Stop! ¡Stop!

17. Read the following Spanish palindromes with the vowel **o**.

O dolor o lodo	Ojo rojo
Somos o no somos	Oro moro

Phoneme /u/

18. The Spanish /u/ is short and is not diphthongized.

bus	club	ataúd	común
luz	cruz	astur	Jesús
sub	plus	atún	salud
sur	algún	aún	según
sus	almud	azul	virtud
tus	alud	baúl	avestruz

19. Now read the following examples that all have unstressed **us**.

álbum	culebra	jugoso
cactus	cuñado	jurado
campus	curado	lujoso
casus	dudoso	mucoso
cónsul	fulano	nuboso
corpus	fumar	mulato
butaca	gusano	sujeto
cubano	jugaba	rutina

20. Unstressed **u** next to any other vowel becomes a semi-vowel [w].

bueno	neuma	jaula
cuero	cuasi	pausa
duele	cuate	cuida
fuera	guapa	huida
huele	Juana	ruido
Ceuta	suave	ruina
deuda	cauce	suizo
feudo	pausa	cuota
reuma	fauna	asiduo

FINAL EXERCISE:

21. The following sentences were taken from various newspaper articles and other sources. Read them and pay attention to the pronunciation of the vowels.

a. Naseiro acudió acompañado de su hija, que con gestos visibles le indicaba que se calmara, que no insistiera en una declaración o alababa sus palabras.
b. Una mujer de avanzada edad no se atrevía a darle la mano, detalle que advirtió la hija de los Reyes, que se acercó a saludarla, mientras la anciana le alababa su belleza
c Las alteraciones de este tipo se expresan en un lenguaje asintáctico y, por tanto, en muchos casos se llega a la agramaticalidad. Aquí ha lugar la distinción de Chomsky entre aceptabilidad y competencia. Una frase es aceptable si, aun incumpliendo las reglas sintácticas, conserva la posibilidad de transmitir su sentido.
d. Este queso se caracteriza por su forma esférica, con protección antiparasitaria de cera roja exterior. Se fabrica también en España.
e. La sensación de estar caminando atrás en el tiempo era demasiado avasalladora como para dejar fisuras al presente inmediato. Nada de lo que estaba viendo, se le ocurría, pertenecía al presente. Esa naturaleza estaba muerta, y su orden pertenecía a un pasado lejano, sibilínamente infiltrado en su modo de percibir la realidad.[2]
f. Es cierto que se trataba de una figura de la vida policíaca bajacaliforniana que no sólo había investigado la muerte de José Federico Benítez López. Además, tenía en su haber un número importante de averiguaciones y asuntos que lo colocaban como potencial blanco de un número importante, significativo, de pasiones que este fin de semana terminaron por desbordarse segando su vida.
g. Los ex rebeldes iniciaron la entrega del armamento colectivo utilizado en el marco del conflicto armado interno, acto en el cual destacaron ametralladoras, lanzagranadas y artefactos explosivos
h. A través de la frontera con Honduras funcionaba eficientemente un correo con la ciudad de Danlí.

[2] The remaining sections are not in the audio program.

i. Cuando algunos escritores llamados vernáculos utilizaron en nuestro país el tema del indio, el tema del campesino, lo estaban haciendo siempre desde una perspectiva eminentemente elitista.
j. La nueva cultura que debemos construir en Nicaragua tiene que ser una cultura de hondo contenido popular, tiene que ser una cultura eminentemente popular.
k. Las manos del mulato criollo aprendieron a tocar eficientemente no sólo la bandurria y la guitarra sino también el acordeón y el arpa.
l. El arte sirve aquí para embellecer, ennoblecer y dignificar no ya una iglesia o un palacio, sino un gran hotel. Teóricamente, la operación consiste en exponer el arte donde está el público, sin esperar a que éste vaya a su encuentro.
m. Se entiende por retórica al arte del bien decir, de embellecer la expresión de los conceptos, de dar al lenguaje escrito o hablado eficacia para deleitar, persuadir o conmover.
n. Asimismo, la imprescriptibilidad significa que el dominio directo es a perpetuidad, no prescribe nunca.
o. En tal escenario encontramos la revocatoria del poder político, la elección de magistrados de la Función Judicial, la institucionalización de la Comisión Anticorrupción de contralor y fiscal, la institucionalización de la Comisión Anticorrupción, etc.
p. La ministerial debe gozar del don de la invisibilidad, porque nadie en Palmar de Ocoa se atreve a asegurar que ella dice la verdad.
q. Usufructo y uso: El carácter vitalicio de estos derechos reales menores determina que la titularidad de los mismos se extinga con la muerte del usufructuario o usuario y, además, estos derechos no son transmisibles por causa de muerte.
r. Para ello parte de la definición de "denotativo" como el "conjunto de las informaciones que vehicula una unidad lingüística y que le permiten entrar en relación con un objeto extra-lingüístico, durante los procesos onomasiológico (denominación) y semasiológico (extracción de sentido e identificación del referente).

13
Linking Spanish Words

IN SPANISH, IF PHONETIC rules allow, the last sound of a word is linked to the first sound of the following word to form a new syllable. This linking is obviously not possible at the end of a phrase or sentence (i.e., where there are commas, periods, or other breaks in one's speech). Consonants at the end of a word are always linked to the vowel that starts the following word, the most common combinations being **d, l, n, r, s + vowel.** For example, **al entrar en el edificio** becomes **a-len-tra-re-ne-le-di-fi-cio; jugar al ajedrez** becomes **ju-ga-ra-la-je-drez; las águilas en el aire** becomes **la-sá-gui-la-se-ne-lai-re; un árbol en España** becomes **u-nár-bo-le-nes-pa-ña.** When two like consonants come together, they fuse into one sound: **el libro** [ɛlíβɾo], **en Navarra** [ɛnaβára].

When a vowel at the end of a word is in contact with a vowel that begins another word, one of three things can happen, all of them pretty logical. When a weak vowel (unstressed **u** or **i**) is in contact with a strong vowel (**a, e, o** or a *stressed* **i** or **u**) a diphthong is created, as in **la-unión** [aw], **mi-amigo** [ya], **la tribu-amazónica** [wa].

Look at the box below. If you are speaking slowly, you might articulate two pure vowels as in the *slow* column; but in normally paced speech you'll articulate them as diphthongs, as in the *fast* column.

	SLOW	RAPID
mi amor	[miamɔ́r]	[myamɔ́r]
mi era	[miɛ́ɾa]	[myɛ́ɾa]
y Ana	[iána]	[yána]
y ojo	[ióxo]	[yóxo]
tu amor	[tuamɔ́ɾ]	[twámɔ́ɾ]
tu era	[tuɛ́ɾa]	[twɛ́ɾa]
tu ojo	[tuóxo]	[twóxo]
tu hija	[tuíxa]	[twíxa]
mi uña	[miúɲya]	[myúɲya]

When two strong vowels **(a, e, o)** are in hiatus—that is, when they are next to each other—they count as two syllables,[3] as in **la única-experiencia** [ae], **entró-en la casa** [oe], **hablé-alemán** [ea].

la era	[laɛ́ɾa]
la hora	[laɔ́ɾa]
fue otro	[fweótɾo]
fue Ana	[fweána]
lo era	[loɛ́ɾa]
lo han	[loán]
le era	[lɛ́ːɾa]

When there are two *unstressed* vowels together, they fuse into a short version of the *second* vowel: **Hable-en español** [áβlenspaɲyól], **la Alhambra** [lalámbɾa]; if one of the like vowels is *stressed*, the resulting fused vowel is lengthened (shown with a kind of modified colon: aː, eː, iː, oː, uː). Compare **Juan le lee** [leléː] with **Léele** [léːle].

This linking of words produces the typical rhythm and pitch of spoken Spanish, characterized by the dominance of open syllables (syllables ending in vowels), which sometimes makes it difficult for foreigners to understand utterances, and gives the impression that the language is spoken very rapidly.

EXERCISES

1. Read the following sentences slowly and pay attention to the linking of words. In this exercise, use slashes (/) to show where syllables begin where words are linked together. Circle the hiatus and the fusion of vowels between words.

a. Eso no se le olvida a nadie. Pero ya tendría él que estar aquí. Mi último recuerdo de su esposa fue el de una noche de grandes lluvias.
b. En ella la exorcizó una hechicera.

[3] Mexicans tend to pronounce **-ear,** as in **pasear** (three syllables) as **-iar,** making is into the diphthongized **pasiar** (two syllables).

c. No era una bruja convencional sino una mujer simpática.
d. Con el último esfuerzo que hizo.
e. El habla hasta su última hora.
f. Como a última hora no encontramos a nadie.
g. ... y en menos de media hora habíamos llegado a una conclusión.
h. ... y el mismo día y a la misma hora en que puse el punto final a estas memorias.

2. Now do the same with the following sentences taken from Colombian newspapers.

a. La última vez que un gobierno se vio obligado a aplicar la dictadura fiscal fue en mil novecientos ochenta y siete.
b. En esa ocasión, el proyecto no pasó en las cámaras legislativas por la oposición que le hizo el Partido Conservador al Gobierno de ese momento.
c. Sin embargo, a la hora de observar la participación sobre el total, el crecimiento no es grande.
d. El saldo en rojo de este año ya va en más de veinte millones de pesos.
e. El club acogió el puerto cundimarqués como sede y esta es la hora en que nadie ha respondido a las expectativas.
f. Ese dinero corresponde a la diferencia entre lo que le cuesta a un exportador comprar el café en el país y lo que recibe a la hora de cambiar por pesos los dólares que le pagan por cada saco.
g. Numerosas atenciones se han ofrecido en honor de Elena Hosie Acevedo.
h. Su voz es bastante melodiosa que se ajusta a los temas con el suave ritmo antillano, con la estructura balada básica o con deliciosos interludios de saxo que le dan ese saborcito a jazz que presenta en algunas canciones.
i. Está ubicado en una de las zonas más costosas del mundo, a unos pasos del área hotelera más cara de Nueva York.
j. Fabio Parra se encuentra en el otro extremo.

3. Once again, do the same with the following text about Colombia.

COLOMBIA

La República de Colombia está ubicada en el noroeste de Sudamérica, limita al norte con Panamá y el mar Caribe, al este con Venezuela y Brasil, al sur con Perú y Ecuador, y al oeste con el océano Pacífico. Colombia es el único país de América del Sur con costas tanto en el océano Atlántico como en el océano Pacífico.

El elemento topográfico más característico de Colombia es la cordillera de los Andes, situada en la parte central y occidental del país, que se extiende de norte a sur a través de casi toda su longitud.
Colombia es el primer exportador mundial de esmeraldas y tiene otras reservas minerales considerables. El café es el cultivo principal. Después de Brasil, Colombia es el segundo productor mundial y el primero en la producción de café suave. Otras industrias destacadas son las dedicadas a la elaboración de alimentos, productos de tabaco, hierro y acero, y equipos de transporte, así como la industria editorial. Los productos químicos están adquiriendo un auge creciente, así como el calzado, la industria textil y la petrolífera.

El idioma oficial es el español pero se hablan más de sesenta dialectos indígenas, que provienen de varias familias lingüísticas.

14
Rhythm

ALL WORDS SPOKEN BETWEEN two pauses—represented, for example, by punctuation marks in writing or by silence in speaking—form a phonetic phrase.

Each phonetic phrase has its own rhythm, characterized by stress and, where English is concerned, length of vowels. In English, as you already know, there are long and short vowels, whereas in Spanish, vowel length is pretty much the same for all vowels, stressed or unstressed.

In English, some vowels are stressed more than others. The stress pattern in the word **responsibility**, for example, can be described as follows:

3		2		3		1		3		3
r e	**s**	**p o**	**n s**	**i**	**b**	**i**	**l**	**i**	**t**	**y**

1 = primary stress
2 = secondary stress
3 = unstressed

In Spanish, things are much easier: a vowel is either stressed or not (and there's no secondary stress); and all vowels have roughly the same length. In the word **Atacama**, for example, there are four [a] sounds, pronounced the same way, and only one is stressed:

1		1		2		1
A	**t**	**a**	**c**	**a**	**m**	**a**

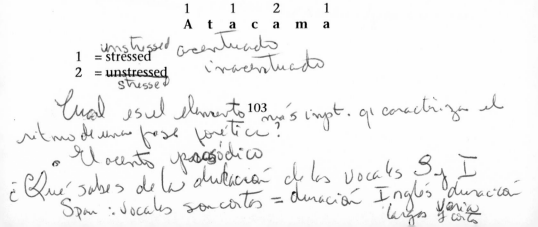

1 = stressed
2 = unstressed

Because there is no secondary vocalic stress in Spanish, it may sound a bit flat to English speakers. The problem is that English speakers want to use secondary stress and long and short vowels, which is only natural, but you should try to avoid English rhythmic patterns in Spanish.

Not every word has a stressed vowel in Spanish, but it's easy to tell which words are stressed. Words that give meaning to the language, the "lexical" words, are stressed—most notably nouns (and their modifiers, adjectives): **casa blanca**; verbs (and their modifiers, adverbs): **fuimos ayer**; as well as question words: **¿quién?** subject pronouns: **usted**; and pronouns that are objects of prepositions: **cerca de ti**; "long possessives": **tuyo, suyo; sí** and **no** (when it means "no") and maybe a couple of other categories. "Grammatical words"—words that give structure to the language—are generally unstressed. These include articles: **el perro**; "short possessives": **mi padre**; direct and indirect object pronouns: **se lo dimos**; the verbs **ser/estar** when they link things together: **yo no soy el presidente, mi padre está enfermo**; prepositions: **cerca de mí**; **no** when it means "not": **No, no lo llamé**, and maybe a few other categories.

Lewis Carroll, in *Through the Looking-Glass*, wrote that poem called "Jabberwocky," whose meaning escaped Alice, even though you can tell the function of every word, because the grammatical words identify its part of speech: " 'Twas brillig, and the slithy toves / Did gyre and gimble in the wabe: / All mimsy were the borogoves, / And the mome raths outgrabe." " 'Twas" indicates that an adjective or **-ing** form of a verb follows. Here there's no **-ing**, so it has to be an adjective. In "the slithy toves" English word order insists that the adjective precede the noun in this circumstance. "All" is an intensification word, showing that an adjective or an adverb follows (here is has to be an adjective). And so on. All the grammatical words here are unstressed, and the "lexical" words—words that give meaning—are the stressed ones.

el acento prosódico En inglés (primario, secundario y sílabas inacentuadas; *Todas las palabras q' dan sentido léxico a la frase son acentuados (nombres, adjet. verbos, adverbios, palabras interrogativas...

EXERCISES

1. Read the following sentences taken from various sources, mark the stress syllables, and pay special attention to the pronunciation of the cognate words.

a. Tras dos días de intensos debates, salpicados de animosidad y resentimiento, el congreso socialdemócrata aprobó, por doscientos sesenta y ocho votos contra veintiocho, la fusión con los liberales.

b. Razón de sobra para que ninguna ley pueda ser objeto de "interpretaciones subjetivas," pues con ello se abre una vía franca para el autoritarismo, el despotismo y la arbitrariedad.

c. El sistema garantiza todas las necesidades de seguridad relacionadas con el cifrado de documentos, la autenticidad de los intervinientes y la certificación del contenido o la fecha de emisión de los correspondientes documentos.

d. Sigamos con el tema del placer. Desde el ángulo de la bioelectricidad, cuanto más abrupta sea la caída de potencial, mayor es la sensación de placer.

e. Según los datos del Parlamento de Quito, la medida propuesta por el Gobierno español supondría el regreso de entre ciento cincuenta mil y doscientos mil súbditos ecuatorianos, que en la actualidad viven y trabajan en la clandestinidad en España.

f. Según los priístas, debe haber compatibilidad entre los programas de Operación Política y el de Elecciones, por lo que pondrán especial énfasis en la organización de mujeres, jóvenes, diputados, organización electoral y líderes sociales.

g. El tiempo mínimo de disponibilidad de ambulancia es de cinco minutos y el máximo de setenta minutos.

h. ¡Remedios, mujer! Estoy hablando en general. España va muy retrasada con respecto a la nueva espiritualidad del mundo y así seguirá mientras a los maestros no se les eleve a la categoría moral que les corresponde, mientras no se les dé el rango social que se merecen.

i. Hablar para arriba, o sólo desde arriba, favorece la generalización, la frustración y la incredibilidad.

j. Lo significativo de la cuestión fiscal hay que buscarlo más bien en la vulnerabilidad que incorpora en las finanzas públicas la dependencia de éstas respecto al capital financiero nacional e internacional.

k. En África, sin ir más lejos, existen grandes potencialidades para la generación de hidroelectricidad, pero su localización las mantiene aún, y quizá por mucho tiempo, inexplotadas.

2. Read the following article, and determine the stress patterns.

EL DESIERTO DE ATACAMA

Una quinta parte de la superficie terrestre está ocupada por desiertos. Pero pocos de ellos concuerdan con la imagen tópica de un mar de dunas que se desplazan a merced de los vientos.
En el desierto chileno de Atacama las erupciones del volcán Parinacota causaron la emergencia de lagos en cuyas riberas crecen unas extrañas vegetaciones adaptadas a las condiciones brumosas, además de grandes lagos salados y géiseres a cuatro mil trescientos veintiún metros de altitud.

Habitado por pueblos indígenas herederos de las extinguidas camanchacas, proanches y atacameños, los aymarás del altiplano han asimilado un modo de vida basado en la cría de llamas y alpacas y el cultivo de maíz y patata.

Este espacio extremo, acaso el más árido del planeta, ofrece oportunidades para la práctica de deportes de aventura, senderismo y rutas a caballo entre los volcanes más altos del Cono Sur.

15
Intonation

A CRITICAL ELEMENT THAT shapes the meaning of an utterance is its intonation. Look at how different the intonation is for these several sentences, which look the same (except for the question mark on the last one).

> *I* ate the sandwich (my brother didn't).
> I *ate* the sandwich (I didn't throw it away).
> I ate the *sandwich* (not the candy bar).
> I ate the sandwich? (What do you mean? I wasn't even near it).

Or "What's that up in the road ahead?" "What's that up in the road? A head?"

In English as in Spanish only three pitch levels are commonly used, a high level (3), a neutral level (2), and a low level (1). A very high pitch level (4) is only used in situations that are charged with emotion.

The most common intonation patterns are to indicate that an utterance is a statement, a question (and what kind of question), or an exclamation.

1. Ordinary statement: used to present facts, descriptions, opinions, etc.

In Spanish, the intonation starts low (1) and raises to the standard level when reaching the first stressed syllable. If the first syllable is *already stressed*, the intonation starts at the neutral level (2). After the *last stressed syllable*, the tone falls to the low level (1). again, unless that syllable is stressed, in which case it stays at level 2.

3
2
1 **Juan lo hi** ~~~~ **zo.**

3 2 1 Tu padre lo hizo.

3 2 1 Mi hermano lo hizo.

3 2 1 El otro profesor nos lo explicó.

3 2 1 El niño juega bajo los árboles.

3 2 1 Comiendo entra la gana.

3 2 1 La risa es el mejor remedio.

3 2 1 Ella se lo llevó.

3 2 1 Lo que es moda no incomoda.

2. Ordinary information question: questions that start with a question word. The intonation curve is the same as for ordinary statements:

3 2 1 ¿Dónde está el salón de clase?

3 2 1 ¿Con quién has ido a la fiesta?

3. Yes or no questions: question that you can answer with "yes" or "no." Instead of descending at the end, the intonation curve raises to 3 at the end, *whether the last syllable is stressed or not:*

3 **se?**
2 **¿Vas al salón de cla**
1

3 **mí?**
2 **tás hablando a**
1 **¿Me es**

The patterns just mentioned are the basic intonation curves in Spanish. All of them have emphatic variations (to express surprise or to emphasize a word). Emphasis is expressed by raising the last stressed syllable in Spanish to the next higher level (3).

4. Emphatic statement. You will see that it takes a bit of conversation for an emphatic statement to develop. Here, the emphatic statement is in the last line.

3
2 **ré a Car**
1 **Pregunta los.**

¿Qué dijiste?

Preguntaré a Carlos.

Preguntarás a quién?

3 **Car**
2 **ré a**
1 **Pregunta los.**

5. Emphatic information question. Again, it takes a while to cause an emphatic question.

3
2 **¿Dónde está la sala de cla**
1 **se?**

¿Dónde está la sala de qué?

3 **cla**
2 **¿Dónde está la sala de**
1 **se?**

6. Emphatic yes-or-no question. In the emphatic yes-or-no question the intonation curve descends to 1 at the end.

¿Vas a la sala de clase?

3
2
1 **¿Vas a la sala de cla** **se?**

No lo puedo creer—

3
2
1 **¿Tú vas la sala de** **cla** **se?**

7. Choice question. As the name suggests, this question asks for a choice. The intonation curve is a combination of an ordinary yes-or-no question and a simple statement:

3
2
1 **¿Quieres ir al ci** **ne** **o** **al tea** **tro?**

8. Echo question. This is a question that only repeats what someone has said, without adding any information, but usually expresses the listener's reaction to the question (for example surprise or discontent, anger, sarcasm, etc.). This kind of question always starts with the unstressed (and meaningless) conjunction **que**.

Imagine this situation: there is a fire in a classroom, and all the students are outside of the room. When the instructor arrives and asks: **¿Por qué no están en la sala de clase?** the students answer:

3
2
1 **¿Que por** **qué no estamos en la sala de cla** **se?**

9. Multiple melodic units in one sentence. Phonetic units, as you know, are separated by pauses. Speakers usually pause after a comma, to take a breath, to think what to say next, or for other reasons. A comma separates clauses, units of meaning, and different parts of an

enumeration. In order to tell the listener that the sentence is not finished yet, speakers don't lower their voice after the last stressed syllable and even raise it slightly. (The slash (/) indicates a pause.):

3
2 ista no entiende su acento, / ted puede señalar el
1 Si el tax us

3
2 nombre de la calle que busca / je
1 en una tar ta.

10. Enumerations. Enumerations in a sentence can be viewed as several shortened statements: **Juan quiere que compres panecillos, tomates y aceite. = Quiere que compres pan. + Quiere que compres tomates. + Quiere que compres aceite.** So each element of an enumeration is treated as if it were a complete clause. Only the next-to-last item is a little different. It stays at the neutral level 2 to indicate that there is only one more item left.

3
2 Juan quiere que compres paneci ma jugo cei
1 llos, to tes, y a te.

11. Exclamations and commands. These have the same intonation curve as normal statements, but the last stressed syllables are louder and higher than in normal statements (it can raise to level 4), to call the attention of the listener.

4 mi 4 cá!
3 3
2 ¡Ven con 2 ¡Ven a
1 go! 1

4 co
3
2
1 ¡So rro!

4 ño 4 Dios!
3 3
2 2 ¡Gracias a
1 !Se ra! 1

12. Greetings and other useful expressions.

3 2 1 Gra cias. De na da.

3 2 1 Por fa vor.

3 2 1 Per dó neme. Lo sien to.

3 2 1 Buenos dí as.

3 2 1 Buenas tar des. Buenas no ches.

3 2 1 ¿Cómo se llama us ted?

3 2 1 ¿Cómo está us ted? Es toy bien, gra cias.

3 2 1 Ho la.

3 2 1 A dios. (standard) 3 2 1 Adio s. (emphatic)

There is a very relation between intonation, stress, pitch and rhythm. Stressed syllables are louder and tend to have a higher pitch than unstressed syllables. Therefore, even though most Spanish speech acts are uttered at an intermediate level (2), stressed syllables stand out, which produces the typical staccato rhythm of Spanish.

EXERCISES

1. Read the following dialogue taken from the play *El Día de la Madre* aloud with a partner. You don't need to read the stage directions.

EL DIA DE LA MADRE

La acción, en Madrid. Época actual.

El primer acto transcurre en el día de la Madre, el 5 de mayo de 1969.
Al comenzar la comedia son las dos de la tarde. La acción, en casa de Teresa. Hace buen tiempo, es primavera en Madrid. No hace frío y empieza a hacer calor.

ACTO PRIMERO
CUADRO PRIMERO

Al levantarse el telón, no hay nadie en escena. En la mesa del comedor está puesto un mantel de hilo bordado. Después de una pequeña pausa, sale del cuarto de la izquierda ANTONIA, *criada de la casa, de unos cincuenta años, lleva unos platos en las manos.*

ANTONIA ¡Señora!... ¡Señora!... ¡Un telegrama!

TERESA (*Dentro*) ¿Cómo dices?.. No te oigo.

ANTONIA ¡Que ha venido un telegrama para usted!

TERESA (*Dentro*) Bueno, no grites tanto... Se van a enterar los vecinos.

ANTONIA (*Pone la mesa.*) Sí, claro..., y si no grito, no me oye... (*Del cuarto de la derecha sale* TERESA, *que se está acabando de vestir.*)

TERESA Anda, ayúdame..., súbeme la cremallera... (*Lo hace.*) Qué, ¿cómo me encuentras?

ANTONIA Nerviosa. Ya es el tercer vestido que se pone.

TERESA ¿Qué hora es?

ANTONIA Van a dar las dos.

TERESA ¡Las dos ya!... No es posible. Óyeme, Antonia.. ¿Tú has visto el collar de perlas?

ANTONIA Sí, señora; lo lleva usted puesto.

TERESA ¡Ah! Sí. Te digo que hoy no tengo la cabeza para nada. Pero... ¿qué estás haciendo aquí?... ¡Ah! Sí, la mesa... Ya tenía que estar puesta. Seis cubiertos, ya sabes... Yo distribuiré los sitios. ¿Huele a quemado...?

ANTONIA No; es el perfume ése, que...

TERESA Sí, es cierto. Oye, Antonia: ¿qué hora es?... No me lo digas, que me muero. Óyeme: a los cubiertos de plata les falta un tenedor de postre, pónmelo a mí.

ANTONIA Si falta, ¿cómo se lo voy a poner?

TERESA ¡Ay, Antonia! me entiendes perfectamente. ¿Qué me iba yo a...? ¡Ah! Sí, los zapatos... Vamos, mujer, date prisa. (*Hace mutis.*)

ANTONIA (*Que sigue poniendo los cubiertos.*) Señora, desde hace dos horas trato de decirle que ha venido un telegrama.

TERESA (*Off.*) ¿Sí?... ¿De quién?

ANTONIA No lo he abierto.

TERESA Mejor. Los telegramas no se deben abrir... Siempre son malas noticias.

ANTONIA ¿Qué hago entonces?... ¿Lo rompo?...

TERESA Lo mejor es que leas lo que pone..., pero no me digas nada. Luego, me bastará con mirarte a los ojos. Tú no puedes engañarme.

ANTONIA Muy bien, señora. A usted la pongo en el sitio de siempre, ¿no?

TERESA Sí. Esa costumbre ¡no se debe romper nunca, para no desconcertar a los invitados. (*Sale del cuarto* TERESA *con otro vestido distinto.*) A ver... ¿Dónde está el telegrama? ¿Lo has abierto?

ANTONIA No, señora... Aquí está

TERESA Trae. (*Lo abre.*)

ANTONIA Pero ése fue el primer vestido que se puso la señora.

TERESA ¡Ah!... ¿Sí?... Ya decía yo. (*Lee el telegrama.*) Antonia... Es de Félix.

ANTONIA No puede venir, seguro; ya lo estaba yo viendo. (*Sigue con la mesa.*)

TERESA Escucha, escucha... Es de Ibiza. «Felicidades, mamá. Llegamos Eva y yo para la comida. Besos. Félix.» Qué, ¿qué te parece?

ANTONIA ¿Y quién es Eva... ?

TERESA No sé... Aquí lo dice.

ANTONIA Le pongo un cubierto?

TERESA ¿Y si es un perro?

ANTONIA Puede ser un amigo.

TERESA Sí..., pon otro cubierto. Es más sencillo quitarlo que ponerlo. Claro que podía especificarlo más.

ANTONIA ¿No será Eva... ?

TERESA ¿Y quién es Eva?

ANTONIA Podía ser una novia del señorito.

TERESA No digas tonterías. Me lo hubiera dicho. Cómo me va a traer a casa, un día como el de hoy... a una novia. Los tiempos han cambiado, pero no tanto. Antonia...

2. Now rewrite these dialogues using three lines for each utterance. Write the parts that are at the neutral level on the middle line, those that are low on the bottom line, and those that are high on the top line.

EN UNA AGENCIA DE VIAJES

AGENTE: Buenos días. ¿En qué puedo ayudarle?

3 --

2 --

1 --

CLIENTE: Buenos días. Yo quiero hacer un viaje a Puerto Rico.

3 --

2 --

1 --

Necesito billetes y otra información.

3 --

2 --

1 --

AGENTE: Bueno. Usted necesita un billete de ida y vuelta ¿verdad?

3 --

2 --

1 --

¿Cuando quiere salir?

3 --

2 --

1 --

CLIENTE: Quiero llegar a San Juan el tres de agosto

3 --

2 --

1 --

y quedarme todo el mes.

3 --

2 --

1 --

AGENTE: Un boleto de avión de Nueva York a San Juan

3 --

2 --

1 --

en segunda clase cuesta trescientos pesos.

3 --

2 --

1 --

CLIENTE: Está bien.

3 --

2 --

1 --

AGENTE: Confirmaré las reservaciones

3

2

1

y le e llamaré por teléfono mañana.

3

2

1

CLIENTE: Perfecto. Muchas gracias.

3

2

1

AGENTE: A sus órdenes.

3

2

1

EN EL AEROPUERTO

FERNANDO: ¡Mamá, papá! ¡Hola! Llegaron por fin.

3

2

1

¿Necesitan ayuda con las maletas?

3

2

1

MADRE: Fernando, ¿qué tal todo? ¿Cómo te va?

3 --

2 --

1 --

FERNANDO: ¿Cómo va todo en Chile?

3 --

2 --

1 --

¿Las casas sobrevivieron el terremoto reciente?

3 --

2 --

1 --

MADRE: Por lo menos, sí.

3 --

2 --

1 --

FERNANDO: Madre, tú te pareces muy joven. ¿Cuántos años tienes?

3 --

2 --

1 --

MADRE: ¡Pues, sigues con las bromas!

3 --

2 --

1 --

¿Cómo está la vida aquí en Colombia?

3

2

1

FERNANDO: Todo bien. ¿Cómo fue el vuelo?

3

2

1

PADRE: Es un viaje bastante largo porque el avión va por Quito

3

2

1

antes de llegar a Bogotá.

3

2

1

FERNANDO: Entonces, necesitamos poner las maletas en el carro

3

2

1

y salir para la casa donde puedan descansar.

3

2

1

16
Variation

In the previous lessons have learned a kind of Spanish pronunciation that is used by a majority of speakers from the urban middle class living in the southern part of Spain as well as most urban areas in Mexico and South America (especially in the north).

In this chapter you are going to learn about some major variations from this "norm," so you won't be surprised when you listen to someone from Castile, from the Caribbean (Cuba, Puerto Rico and the Northern Coast of Colombia and Venezuela), or from the southern part of South America (for example, Argentina and Uruguay), because, as with English, people from different places pronounce the language in different ways. Not only do people speak differently in the various parts of a country, they even speak differently in the same areadepending on their social status (peasants, construction workers, lawyers, priests, etc.) the cultural group (priests, office workers, gauchos) they belong to, and whether they are male or female, old or young. As you can imagine, these variations are endless, and therefore we will only mention the most widespread ones resulting in additional phonetic and phonemic differences.

The Castilian "theta" /θ/:

Pronunciation:	Voiceless interdental fricative, same as the English **th** in **think**, **thin**
Spelling:	z before **a**, **o**, **u** and **c** before **e** , **i**
Transcription:	[θ]
Examples:	**Zaragoza** [θaɾaɣóθa], **zarzuela** [θaɾθwéla], **celebración** [θelebɾaθyón], **cerveza** [θeɾβéθa]

Because this phoneme is non-existent in many parts of Andalusia and in Spanish America, words such as **casa** (house)–**caza** (hunt), **caso** (case)–**cazo** (I hunt), **poso** (I pose)–**pozo** (well), **rosa** (rose)–**roza** (he/she touches), **tasa** (tax)– **taza** (cup) are HOMOPHONES—words with different meanings that sound alike. Only the context distinguishes the meaning. The pronunciation of **c** and **z** as [s] is called **seseo**. When **c** and **z** are pronounced [θ] it is calles **ceceo** [θeθéo].[1]

Castilian tip-of-the-tongue [ș]:	
Pronunciation:	Voiceless alveolar fricative (formed with the tip instead of the upper back of the tongue)
Spelling:	**s**
Transcription:	[ș]
Example:	**casa** [káșa]
Distribution:	Center and northern Spain, including Madrid

The apical **s** is used between vowels, after consonants, before unvoiced consonants (except **t**), and is not used in word-initial position.

The Castilian palatal lateral **ll** [ʎy]:	
Pronunciation:	Voiced palatal lateral sound, a combination of [ʎ]] and [y] similar to the **ll** in **million.**
Spelling:	**ll**
Transcription:	[ʎy]
Example:	**calle** [káʎye]
Distribution:	Parts of Northern Spain.

[1] There is a legend that circulates, mainly in Spanish classes, that a Spanish king had a lisp and ordered his subjects to use the **ceceo**. This is nonsense, since the sound [θ] and [s] exist in the language, and sometimes even side by side: **doscientos, fascinante.**

This sound, once in general use in Spain, has almost disappeared and is not used in Spanish America. It is still used by older speakers in Northern Spain, but sounds already archaic and aristocratic. The consequence of its disappearance is the convergence of the phonetic representation of **ll** and **y**, which means that both words **rayo** *(lightning)* and **rallo** (*I shred*) now sound alike. Other examples are **Maya** (Mayan) – **malla** (mesh) and **vaya** (the subjunctive of **ir**) – **valla** (fence). This phenomenon is almost universal and is called *yeísmo*.

In southern South America this [y] has seen another variation:

The **ll** and **y** in Argentina and Uruguay [ʒ]:	
Pronunciation:	Voiced palatal fricative, like the English **s** in **measure.**
Spelling:	**ll** and **y**
Transcription:	[ʒ]
Examples:	**calle** [káʒe], **rayo** [ráʒo]
Distribution:	Argentina and Uruguay

There is also a tendency among the young people in that region, especially in Buenos Aires, to use [ʃ] (as in **ship**) instead of [ʒ]. How would **Yo soy un paraguayo y me llamo Portillo** sound in young person's speech?

THE WEAKENING OR LOSS OF S AT THE END OF SYLLABLES AND WORDS

A very widespread phenomenon is the weakening and even elimination of the **s** that ends syllables and words, also known as **comerse los eses.** This weakening is common and socially accepted in southern Spain, the Canary Islands, the Caribbean, Central America, and even in the countries of southern South America.

This process has basically five variants:

1. Aspiration of final s: **estas mesas** = [ésta^{h}mésa^{h}].
2. Aspiration of **s** at the end of a syllable: **estas mesas** = [ɛ́^{h}ta^{h} mésa^{h}].
3. Assimilation of the [h] to the following sound: **estas mesas** = [ɛ́^{h}ta̲

m̲ésa^h].[2]

4. Exchange of final **s** with a lengthened sound that starts the next syllable: **casco** = [ká^{k}ko].
5. Elimination of final **s: estas mesas** = [ɛ́^{h}tamésa].

The first variant is without any doubt the most widespread one, whereas the other variants, especially the complete elimination of final **s**, is bound to very specific geographic and social limitations. This means that even in places where the aspiration of final **s** is the norm and socially accepted, the complete elimination might be considered substandard.

You should just be aware of the phenomenon so that you can understand people who pronounce this way when they ask **¿Comoetáuté?**

Spanish is not the only Romance Language that has lost or is losing an **s** that ends a syllable. It happened in French a thousand years ago. Look at **étude, plâtre, île** (Sp. **estudio**, Eng. **plaster**, Sp. **isla**).

THE WEAKENING AND MERGER OF FINAL L AND **R**

Another regional and social variation is the replacement of [r] by [l] or the replacement of both [l] and [ɾ], at the end of syllables. There are very few words that become homophones with this neutralization, for example **harto – alto** [áɾ̪t̪o] or [ál̪t̪o], **Marta** ("Martha") – **Malta** (Malta) [máɾ̪t̪a] or [mál̪t̪a] and **sarta** (row, line) – **salta** (he/she jumps) [sáɾ̪t̪a] or [sál̪t̪a]. We even once overheard a woman address her husband as **mi amol.** You can hear this in many parts of Andalusia, some areas of New Castile, Murcia, Extremadura and southern Salamanca, the Canary Islands, the islands and coastal areas of the Caribbean and the Pacific coast, but even here it is often associated with rural and uncultivated speech.

---

[2] The **s** of **mesa** is not aspirated because it is at the beginning of a syllable.

17
Phonetic Transcription

YOUR COURSE IS ABOUT to end and you still have lots to do and practice before your pronunciation approaches that of a near-native level. How can you be sure that you will not continue old bad habits or that you will not develop new ones? A very good way is to master the transcription of texts into phonetic characters. If you can transcribe a text accurately in phonetic characters, it means that you know exactly how it's supposed to be pronounced, even though it may take you a long time to put all these notions into effect.

Hopefully you will have a couple of weeks left in your course so that you can practice transcriptions of texts—virtually any text will do—as homework, on the overhead projector, or on the blackboard, and have your classmates and instructor critique your work. It is tough at the beginning because there are so many rules to remember, but in time it will become second nature. Some people think it's even fun.

You have seen examples of phonetic texts throughout the book, but it's a good idea to set down the basic rules here. All phonetic texts are written between brackets [ ] to show that it is a *phonetic* transcription and not a *phonemic* transcription (phonemic transcriptions are possible, too, and are written between slashes / /). There are no phonetic capital letters, and there are no spaces between words, just as there are no pauses between words when you speak. Stressed words have accent marks (basically nouns, adjectives, verbs, adverbs, certain pronouns and a few other categories from Chapter 14). Where there are commas and really short breaks, use a slash to separate the clauses. Where there are periods or long breaks use two slashes.

You have to be careful to make transcriptions of the exact sounds that the text implies. This sounds obvious enough, but we have had more than one student who would pronounce the text to *him/herself,* then write the transcription as *he/she* would pronounce it. Interesting linguistic phenomenon, but it doesn't help improve pronunciation.

Another thing to bear in mind is not to be duped by orthographic letters as they appear in the Spanish text, and write the *same* letters in the transcription. The letter **c** sometimes creeps into phonetic transcriptions because there is a **c** in the text (but there is no phonetic character [c]). Sometimes students write a **y**, because there is a **y** in the written text, where an [i] is called for. Similarly, you know that a **z** is typically transcribed [s], and **ch** is transcribed [č], so be careful not to use *orthographic* characters in your *phonetic* transcriptions.

We offer some samples of transcriptions here, taken from exercises seen in the book. For your homework and for use in class, your instructor will provide you with texts.

Sigamos con el tema del placer. Desde el ángulo de la bioelectricidad,
[siɣámoskonɛlt̪émaðɛlplasɛ́ɾ // d̪ézðɛláŋguloðelaβyoelɛkt̪ɾisiðáð /

cuanto más abrupta sea la caída de potencial, mayor es la sensación
kwant̪omásaβɾúpt̪asealakaíðaðepot̪ɛnsyál / mayóɾɛzlasɛnsasyón̪

de placer.
d̪eplasɛ́ɾ]

In the above example, you'll see that a dental **n** ends the next-to-last line because a dental **d** begins the last line. Don't be fooled by end-of-line breaks. Here is a longer example:

Unos cinco mil cocaleros protagonizaron un bloqueo de la principal
[unosíŋkomílkokaléɾospɾot̪aɣonisáɾonumblokéoðelapɾinsipál

ruta de Bolivia, en contra de la proyectada instalación de tres bases
rút̪aðeβolíβya / eŋkón̪t̪ɾaðelapɾoyɛkt̪áðaynst̪alasyón̪d̪et̪ɾezβásez

militares en la convulsa región del Chapare. Los productores comen-
milit̪áɾesɛnlakombúlsarɛxyón̪d̪ɛʎčapáɾe // lospɾoðukt̪ɔ́ɾeskomɛn

zaron el bloqueo de la vía que vincula el eje troncal del país confor-
sáɾonɛlβlokéoðelaβíakeβiŋkúlaɛléxet̪ɾoŋkál̪d̪ɛlpaískoɱfɔɾ

mado por los departamentos de La Paz, Cochabamba y Santa Cruz.
máðopɔrlozðepart̪amɛ́n̪t̪ozðelapás / kočaβámbaysán̪t̪akɾús]

Here is a third example.

El profesor Pérez fue llevado ante el intendente municipal de la ciu-
[ɛlpɾofesɔ́ɾ péɾɛsfweyeβáðoan̪t̪ɛlin̪t̪ɛn̪d̪ɛ́n̪t̪emunisipál̪d̪elasyu

dad de Buenos Aires, Manuel Güiraldes, quien, poco después, lo de-
ðáðeβwénosáyɾes / manwɛ́lɣwiɾál̪d̪es / kyɛ́n / pókoðɛspués / loðe

signó laringólogo honorario del Teatro Colón que aún no se había
siɣnólaɾiŋgóloɣonoɾáyoðɛl̪t̪eát̪ɾokolóŋkeaúnoseβía

inaugurado.
ynawɣuɾáðo]

Pay attention to

n̪ t̪

/

d

ɛ

g

b

s, z

973-534-7394

Printed in the United States
33966LVS00003B/70-117

9 780942 566444